T0065967

BOOZE *Over* BROADWAY

BOOZE *Over* BROADWAY

50 COCKTAILS FOR THEATRE LOVERS

MICHAEL GOFF, RONNIE ALVARADO, AND MICHAEL ANDERSEN

TILLER PRESS

NEW YORK   LONDON   TORONTO   SYDNEY   NEW DELHI

TILLER PRESS

An Imprint of Simon & Schuster, Inc.
1230 Avenue of the Americas
New York, NY 10020

First Tiller Press hardcover edition November 2021

TILLER PRESS and colophon are registered trademarks of Simon & Schuster, Inc.

For information about special discounts for bulk purchases, please contact Simon &
Schuster Special Sales at 1-866-506-1949 or business@simonandschuster.com.

The Simon & Schuster Speakers Bureau can bring authors to your live event.
For more information or to book an event, contact the Simon & Schuster Speakers
Bureau at 1-866-248-3049 or visit our website at www.simonspeakers.com.

Interior design by Matt Ryan
Illustrations by Brandan Leathead

Manufactured in the United States of America

10 9 8 7 6 5 4 3 2 1

Library of Congress Cataloging-in-Publication Data

Names: Goff, Michael, 1965– author.
Title: Booze over Broadway : 50 cocktails for theatre lovers /
recipes by Michael Goff.
Description: First Tiller Press hardcover edition. | New York : Tiller Press, 2021. |
Includes index.
Identifiers: LCCN 2021011767 (print) | LCCN 2021011768 (ebook) |
ISBN 9781982160005 (hardcover) | ISBN 9781982160036 (ebook)
Subjects: LCSH: Cocktails. | Musicals—New York (State)—New York. |
LCGFT: Cookbooks.
Classification: LCC TX951 .G53 2021 (print) | LCC TX951 (ebook) |
DDC 641.87/4—dc23
LC record available at https://lccn.loc.gov/2021011767
LC ebook record available at https://lccn.loc.gov/2021011768

ISBN 978-1-9821-6000-5
ISBN 978-1-9821-6003-6 (ebook)

THE CAST

Ladies and gentlemen, please take your seats– the show is about to start.

AS ANY THEATRE LOVER KNOWS, there's nothing quite like a musical. The lights, the dance numbers, the moving ballads, and captivating choruses: There's something magical about watching the spectacle of it all.

So, to satisfy even the most ardent of Broadway buffs, we've crafted fifty delectable cocktails inspired by some of the greatest musicals of all time. With libations ranging from the tropical "South Pacific Breeze" or "Oh, What a Beautiful Mai Tai," to innovative twists like "The Jelly-cul Choice" or "La Vie Bohemian," to classics like "All that Jack 'n' Coke" to "If I Were a Rich Man(hattan)," we've got drink and show pairings to suit every palate and preference.

Each entry on our playbill includes a brief introduction to the show referenced from a team of lifelong theatre lovers, while each scrumptious recipe has been specially crafted by a rising star in the New York City bar scene, Michael Goff. A Broadway buff himself, our trusty bartender has cultivated a list of jaw-dropping numbers to please even the most demanding of divas, and includes variations, substitutes, and "encores" to elevate the drinks when called for. For readers who may be making their cocktail debut, a list of the referenced barware, mixing methods, spirits, and garnishes is included prior to the recipes. (Please note that all the included descriptions and explanations are based from Michael's expert opinion but should not be interpreted as fact. Further, none of these recipes should be comsumed by any theatre lover under the age of twenty-one.)

Whether you're hosting a Tony Awards watch party, holding a family musical night, or listening to your favorite soundtrack solo, what are you waiting for? Put on your Phantom mask, take a drink, and break a leg!

THE HOWS AND THE WHATS

SOME EXPERT TIPS FROM OUR BARTENDER

Glassware

There are numerous different glassware types and styles but for our purposes, I've kept it to a tidy dozen, with the most essential being given top billing and others rounding out the supporting cast. No need to break the bank on any of these, either. For example, my most prized punch bowl is a thrift-store find, which along with its matching twelve cups cost me a scandalous $14.

However, you may prefer that all your glassware match. If you're planning on outfitting your home bar all at once, a local restaurant supply store is a grand place to start.

COLLINS OR HIGHBALL
11 TO 16 OUNCES

Technically the collins and highball are two different glasses (highball is a bit smaller, shorter, and typically a hair wider). Both glasses fall under the "long drinks" variety and are pressed into use for drinks that are "topped" or "filled" with a nonalcoholic sparkling component, typically a seltzer or soft drink. Collins glasses also make for an excellent Bloody Mary vessel due to their larger overall volume. Both are extremely versatile and photogenic.

COUPE GLASS
5 TO 7 OUNCES

Whether it's martinis, daiquiris, or sours, the coupe is the go-to workhorse of almost any shaken drink served "up." Plus, due to its elegant curved sides, it's a bit easier to keep the liquor where you want it than the straight-sided "cocktail glass."

DOUBLE OLD-FASHIONED
12 TO 14 OUNCES

While a classic single old-fashioned is a fine glass, its somewhat diminutive size makes it less versatile than its brawnier brother. Able to accommodate large-format ice cubes, for most rocks (over ice, that is) drinks that don't get a fizzy finish, the double old-fashioned is the one that I want (oo, oo, oo, honey).

PINT GLASS
16 TO 20 OUNCES

While it may seem odd that a pint glass would be any volume other than 16 ounces, due to a quirk of British law, a "pint" of beer is equal to 20 imperial ounces (or 19.2 US ounces). At any rate, pints are ideal for beers, ciders, and beer-based cocktails, such as shandies. Due to their wide base, cocktails served in a pint glass often provide the opportunity for ever more ambitious garnishes. (Is that a chicken wing on top of that Bloody Mary?) They are durable, relatively inexpensive, and typically stackable.

WINEGLASS (WHITE WINE OR ALL-PURPOSE)
12 OUNCES

When you think of a wineglass, this is probably what comes to mind. Either stemmed or stemless, the volume and shape of an all-purpose wineglass make it suitable for everything from a glass of lovely Chardonnay to an Aperol spritz, and many points in between.

SUPPORTING PLAYERS

CHAMPAGNE FLUTE
6 TO 8 OUNCES

Whether stemmed or stemless, any sparkling wine is better enjoyed by the festive shape of a flute, due to its narrow neck, which prevents the fizz from escaping too quickly.

COCKTAIL GLASS/MARTINI GLASS
5 TO 7 OUNCES

Ah, the classic V-shaped vessel, which of course comes with the connotations of class and power. Unfortunately, the cocktail glass most often seen for sale today is overly large, and due to its shape it has always had a bad habit of causing the holder to wear a bit of the drink. (I don't know about you, but I prefer my cocktails taken internally.) That said, a not-too-big, properly chilled cocktail glass with an ice-cold martini or Gibson inside is indeed a pleasure.

NICK 'N' NORA
4 TO 6 OUNCES

Perhaps the snazziest of all cocktail glasses, the Nick 'n' Nora is a stemmed glass with an inverted bell shape for the bowl. It's perfect for most stirred drinks served up, although I like the slightly larger coupe for shaken drinks. It's my favorite glass to sip something up, mixed, and potent, as it's an elegant shape.

SINGLE OLD-FASHIONED
6 TO 8 OUNCES

The ideal size for neat pours of spirits, the single old-fashioned is small enough to be used for shots but large enough for a rocks pour.

PUNCH BOWL

Just about any large, food-safe container can work as a punch bowl, but to bring out the "wow" factor at your next soiree, a classic bowl makes serving a group a breeze.

SHOT GLASS
¾ TO 2 OUNCES

While shot glasses are a bar staple, at home they can also do double duty as a handy measuring cup if you misplace your jigger or angled measuring cup.

TODDY MUG
8 TO 10 OUNCES

Perfect for just about any hot drink, the defining characteristic of a toddy mug, as opposed to a regular mug, is that they are typically made of glass instead of ceramic. Note: If you see the term "charged mug" in a recipe, just preheat the mug with hot water, then discard it before you add your cocktail.

WINEGLASS (RED)
14 TO 22 OUNCES

The red wine glass can run the gambit of shapes, from relatively small Sauterne glasses to gigantic Burgundy and Bordeaux. While the shape of the glass can impact which aromatic compounds are more or less noticeable when you drink from them, if you're in a pinch for space, the standard wineglass listed above will do just fine. Also, remember dear Broadway buff, just because a glass can hold more liquid doesn't mean it should.

HONORABLE MENTION

THE SOLO CUP

A true staple of many a tailgate, barbecue, picnic, and cookout. Virtually any cold drink can and has been enjoyed out of a SOLO cup. Avoid serving hot beverages in them as you're liable to hurt your hands and the cup can deform due to heat. And, yes, the three lines on the bottom of the cup approximate 1, 5, and 12 ounces, respectively. If your surroundings call for disposable cups, do please recycle.

Barware

To give you a better idea of what you really need for opening night, we've separated the following barware into the essentials (principal performers) and optional equipment (supporting cast). That being said, none of these are absolutely required for any of the libations included. You can certainly craft successful cocktails without these items, just as a great performer can command the stage solo. That being said, musical numbers tend to be a lot more fun with an orchestra and some backup chorus. Additionally, there are workarounds and substitutes sprinkled throughout in case you can't find any of these items.

PRINCIPAL PERFORMERS

JIGGER

One of the keys to good drink making is having consistent measurements. Jiggers, with their set volumes and interior markers, make it easy to pour the right amount every time.

PEELER AND PARING KNIFE

While garnishes (see page 18) may seem to many like an afterthought, when properly applied and with some consideration of function, they should enhance your drinking experience. A peeler will make short work of citrus peels and cucumber ribbons, while a paring knife will handle just about everything else.

STRAINER

Key for separating ice, muddled ingredients, etc., from prepared cocktails. If you can only have one, make it a Hawthorne strainer. The wire coil is easily cleaned and ensures the strainer will fit shakers, mixing tins, measuring cups, and the like. Additionally, a 4-inch, conical fine-mesh strainer is a great thing to add to any bar kit.

SHAKER

An absolute workhorse that no home bar should go without. The cocktail shaker comes in basically two iterations.

BOSTON SHAKER Two pieces, 12 ounces on one side, 28 ounces on the other. While tin-on-glass is an option, they are more prone to leaks. The tin-on-tin style is the pro's choice for a reason. They can take a little time to master, but a good set of tins will last years.

COBBLER SHAKER Three pieces, large tin, top with built-in strainer, and cap. The cobbler does have the advantage over the Boston, as its strainer is built right in, but the caps are prone to getting stuck and can be tricky to clean. Great for home bartenders. If you're in a pinch, a "blender cup," usually used for protein powder shakes, makes a handy stand-in.

SUPPORTING CAST

While all these are definitely nice to have, you can make a majority of the recipes without them.

BARSPOON

Whether it's effortlessly stirring a Negroni, fishing a cherry out of a jar to garnish a Manhattan, cracking an ice cube, or adding a very small amount of an ingredient to a recipe, a good barspoon is well worth its weight. The distinctive spiral shape of the handle is useful for layering drinks, and with a little practice it aids the stirring motion. A 12-inch model (holds approximately 2.5 milliliters) is ideal for the home bar. If you don't have one, use an iced-tea spoon. Don't have that? Grab a chopstick.

BLENDER

Useful for both whipping up a pitcher of frozen drinks and preparing batched ingredients to be used later. A good blender should be sturdy and have enough power to easily crush ice cubes.

CHANNEL KNIFE

A specially shaped garnish cutting tool made to easily cut long ribbons of citrus peel.

GRATER AND MICROPLANE

Nothing says "Drink me, I'm delicious" quite so much as a little freshly grated nutmeg on a Dark 'n' Stormy or cinnamon on a hot toddy, and nothing grates as quickly and neatly as a microplane.

ICE TRAYS AND MOLDS

One of the biggest differences between drinks made in cocktail bars versus home bars is the quality of the ice. While the hard plastic trays that came with your fridge will do the job, swapping them out for a few quality ice molds will quickly improve your drink game. There's a wide variety of fun-shaped molds out there, but the two most useful ones are the 1¼-inch and 2-inch cube trays. Also referred to respectively as the "perfect" and "king cube."

PRO TIP Store your ice cubes in a zippered bag or similar so they don't end up picking up funky-fridge odors. You don't want tonight's Tom Collins tasting like last night's mac and cheese.

JUICER

Besides good-quality ice, using fresh citrus juice in your cocktails will do wonders for just about any cocktail that calls for it. Don't have one handy? Use your hands and be sure to strain out any seeds.

MIXING GLASS

While stirred drinks can certainly be prepared in the large tin of your shaker, a mixing glass has some definite advantages. Due to its wider base, it's both easier to stir drinks in and less likely to tip over. Tight on space? Use a 2-cup measuring cup. Julia Child did it and she made a mean martini.

MUDDLER

While you can make do with a wooden spoon to occasionally bruise mint leaves for a mojito or crush a few berries, when it comes to sturdier items like sugar cubes or cucumber slices, a proper muddler will make your hands a whole lot happier.

Techniques

While it may seem intimidating at first, with a little practice you'll be shaking like a train and smoothly pouring like a pro. As with any fine-motor skill, be ready to adapt. If you find it hard to fill a jigger to the full 2 ounces and then get all of those ounces into your tin or mixing glass, then start with pouring 1½ ounces, then a ½-ounce measure.

BUILD

Very common among highballs and warm drinks, a "built-in-glass" cocktail is about as straightforward as it gets. That said, there are a few tips to ensure a consistent cocktail. For a spirit, plus carbonated mixer (think scotch highball, gin and tonic, vodka soda, etc.), it can be helpful to add a splash of the mixer into the glass first before you add the spirit(s). This will ensure better integration of booze(s) and mixer without having to stir the cocktail too much and will knock out any carbonation. For drinks with big garnishes that take up space in the glass—celery stalks, for example—it can be a good idea to insert the garnish in with the ice before building the drink.

MUDDLE

Whether using a proper muddler, a dowel, or a wooden spoon, there is a bit of method to the smashing. Add your ingredient to be muddled with whatever sweetener is going in the cocktail. Then hold the muddler in your dominant hand, press down firmly on the contents, and give it a little twist. Continue to press, twist, press, twist like a Baltimore teenager in *Hairspray*. Be sure to muddle the sturdiest ingredients first. For example, if you plan to make a Royal Ascot, first muddle the raspberries, then add bitters, and finally simple syrup. For fresh herbs, you need only muddle until you can smell them wafting from the tin, and you'll be a star.

RIM

Spread a little of your rim ingredient on a small plate. Next, take your chilled glassware and, using the side of a piece of citrus, wet the outer rim of the glass. Then roll or dab the lip of the glass in your rimming ingredient. When preparing for guests, it's good etiquette to only rim half the glass so the recipients may choose whether they want the added seasonings or not.

SHAKE

Perhaps the most debated technique among professional bartenders, a good shake for a home bartender needs, above all, to be consistent.

If you're using solid cubes (like from ice cube trays/molds), follow the recipe instructions as written. If you're using the ice found in most home fridge ice makers, shorten your shake so you don't overdilute your cocktails. If you're using "shell ice" from most hotel or convenience stores, only give three or four shakes to incorporate the drink, since it will dilute very quickly.

Regardless of shaker type, once you have your ingredients and ice all sealed up, please don't shake your drinks like you're churning butter. An up-and-down motion won't aerate and open up your cocktail nearly as well as holding the sealed container sideways. If your hands will allow it, a single-hand shake should look a little like an American football "pump-fake," but repeated for as long as it takes for the tin to get very cold. If shaking with two hands, keep the tin in front of your sternum with one hand on each tin as you repeatedly shake away and toward your body. Once the tin is very cold in your hands, set it on a counter, larger side down, hold firmly with one hand, then use your other hand to slap the side of the tin to break the vacuum. With a cobbler shaker, the process is identical, but aim for the cap instead.

STIR

For cocktails that only contain spirits, bitters, and sweeteners, a stirred technique is typically recommended. While the "natural" motion to stir something is often holding the spoon firmly in your hand, then turning your wrist, keep in mind you aren't making pancakes, you're making drinks. Instead, your wrist should stay fairly still as your fingers guide the spoon through the cocktail in a circular motion. Stirred drinks can reach incredibly cold temperatures with minimal dilution and a little bit of technique. While many books and blogs will tell you to stir times in each direction, I have been unable to find any validity to the claim. Instead of counting stirs, I would recommend you count off about fifteen or so seconds while stirring as smoothly as you can. Then strain the cocktail immediately. If you're making multiple drinks in the same glass at the same time, add another ten seconds to your stir to properly dilute and chill the drinks before dividing them.

STRAIN

This is a straightforward technique, but a few hard-won tips will have you looking like a pro. If you have a Hawthorne strainer, now is a great time to master using it. (Just toss a few ice cubes and a half cup of water in the tin—there's no sense wasting liquor when you're learning.) Place your strainer onto the top of your mixing tin spring-side down. Practice pouring into a piece of glassware until you feel comfortable with the weight and feel of the tin. If using a cobbler tin with a built-in strainer, be sure to wiggle the tin a little as you pour to get all of your beverage where it belongs. Have lots of bits of herbs or fruit in your drink? Pour through the regular strainer and through a fine-mesh strainer perched or held over your glassware.

Spirits

Our bartender could go on for lengths about spirits, but we promise to keep it brief, highlighting the "one singular sensation" about each of the booze types included. This is not meant to be definitive, merely an informative introduction.

AMARO

A collection of often-but-not-always Italian bitter liqueurs originally meant as restoratives, aperitifs, or digestifs. Campari, Averna, Cynar, and Fernet-Branca are all great examples, but this is an incredibly diverse category, so our best advice is to taste as many as you can as often as you can.

APPLEJACK

Though technically a member of the brandy category below, applejack's importance in American spirits is too large not to give it its own entry. (Plus, it's called for in a few recipes.) The oldest-known distilled spirit in North America, applejack is made from fermenting the juice of pressed apples into hard cider, then distilling it into a liquor. Modern applejack is distilled in the same manner. Aged examples compare favorably with the finest spirits in the world.

BEER

Almost assuredly the oldest produced alcoholic beverage in the world, beer contains dozens, if not hundreds, of different recognized styles today. Beer owes its diversity to changing variables like grains, hops, and boil times, as well as the additions of various flavorings like spices, citrus, and coffee.

BRANDY

While brandy is typically thought of as any distilled spirit made primarily from fruit instead of grain, it is considered to be "hot" or "boozy" at a young age but will develop incredible depth of flavor when aged. As a diverse spirit used heavily in classic cocktails, brandy has earned its place on this list.

GIN

Gin is generally considered the oldest recognized distilled spirit in the world. Its defining characteristic is a grain-based liquor flavored with juniper berries, along with any number of other ingredients. The category has innumerable variants, but the best-known are listed below:

LONDON DRY: When you think gin you're probably thinking of a London dry. Typically more than 85 proof and predominantly flavored with juniper berries, it is one of the most frequently used spirits in the world.

SLOE: Sloe gin is made by infusing or distilling gin with the sloe berry, giving it a sweet, slightly softened, and decidedly fruit-forward flavor.

WESTERN: Typically a bit less boozy than its London cousin, Western-style gins tend to feature a broader base of aromatics beyond just juniper. Citrus plays a popular part in this type along with any number of botanicals or aromatics, like rose hips, cucumber, elderflower, bay leaf, or lavender.

MEZCAL

One of the fastest growing spirits categories, mezcal is essentially tequila's smokier, brawnier brother. Mezcal's distinctly rich mouthfeel and smokiness pair with the gently sweet and peppery agave for a great drink sipped neat or worked into many cocktails.

RUM

While it's an oversimplification, for our purposes we'll talk about the three most prominent styles, plus spiced rum.

JAMAICAN RUM: Distinct from its Caribbean cousins due to its fermentation process, rums from Jamaica tend to have complex fruit flavors ranging from mango tones, to banana-and-baking-spice, to vanilla-and-brown-sugar. It is excellent in tiki cocktails, or with some longer-aged expressions sipped solo like cognac.

WHITE RUM: Unaged and added to make drinks boozier, the majority of well-known white rums hail from the Caribbean and are best used in cocktails like daiquiris and mojitos.

TEQUILA

A much-beloved if often misunderstood category of distilled spirits. Tequila is technically a type of mezcal (see opposite page). It can be handy to remember that all tequilas are mezcal, but not all mezcals are tequila.

AÑEJO: Añejo, or "aged" tequila, is reposado (see below) that has been aged for one to three years. Añejo is typically darker in color and smoother than reposado, with noticeable notes of caramel, oak, and toffee. Often sipped neat, it can be a great swap in for many whiskey cocktails.

BLANCO: Blanco tequila is unaged, and the only additive is water to cut it to a proof no lower than 37.5 percent. With its floral, sweet agave aromas, the flavor is a little peppery with mild hints of vanilla and pineapple.

EXTRA AÑEJO: Also called ultra-aged tequila, it is an añejo that has been aged at least three years. Noticeably darker than other tequilas, its very smooth, faint remnants of peppery agave are joined by notes of caramel, dried fruit, and mildly nutty flavors.

REPOSADO: Reposado or "rested" tequila is blanco tequila that has been rested in oak vessels (most often used bourbon barrels) for two to twelve months. Light amber in color, reposado tequila is usually more mellow than other tequilas, and maintains the peppery agave but with rounder smoother flavors of oak and vanilla. Aromatic herbs can be a great garnish for reposado cocktails in particular.

RHUM AGRICOLE: Rhum hails from the former French colonial areas of the Caribbean. Made from raw sugarcane juice instead of molasses or cooked sugar, rhum agricole tends to taste grassy with a bright alcohol bite and some fun tropical fruit notes like papaya. A favorite of cocktail bartenders for the complexity it brings to drinks.

SPICED RUM: Spiced rums take relatively neutral rums and add warm spices such as cinnamon, clove, nutmeg, allspice, and ginger, plus caramel coloring and a lot of sugar.

VODKA

Classically a blend of ethanol and water, vodka originated in Poland and Russia but is now made around the world. Here in the United States, vodka is no longer seen as being without distinctive aroma, taste, or color, though it still can't be aged in wood and must meet certain manufacturing standards to be legally sold as vodka. The chameleonlike ability of vodka to mix with so many ingredients and its relatively neutral flavor make it a great staple of any home bar. A useful way to think of vodka is as an amplifier. Add if you're happy with the flavor of a drink but need it to pack a bit more of a wallop.

WHĪSKEY

Yet another very popular and diverse category of distilled spirits. In terms of a defining characteristic, virtually all whiskey is made from grain, whether it's corn, barley, rye, wheat, rice, sorghum, or amaranth. For the sake of brevity, in addition to bourbon and rye, below are five distinct styles mainly, but not solely, defined by geography. Pro tip: If spelled "whiskey" it is from the United States or Ireland. If spelled "whisky," it's from Scotland, Canada, or Japan.

BOURBON: Distinctly American, to be classified as bourbon it must be made in the United States, contain at least 51 percent corn, be aged in new-charred oak barrels for a minimum of two years, be bottled at least 80 proof, and the only additive can be water for the purposes of adjusting the proof.

CANADIAN WHISKY: To be considered Canadian whisky, the spirit must be mashed, distilled, and aged in Canada, aged in wood barrels for no less than three years, be bottled at least 80 proof, and may contain caramel and flavoring.

IRISH WHISKEY: Smooth, light, and with hints of fruit and grain, Irish whiskey is renowned for its easy drinkability. To qualify as Irish whiskey, it must be made in Ireland, made predominantly with barley, distilled to no higher than 189 proof, aged in Ireland for a minimum of three years, and cannot contain any additives other than water and caramel coloring.

JAPANESE WHISKY Historically, Japanese whisky has been an expression of master blenders importing whisk(e)y from all over the world to create a typically light, delicate, and sweet style of whisky. At the time of this writing, a new set of proposed standards for Japanese whisky has been published but not yet agreed to or ratified.

RYE Distinct from its blended Canadian cousin, rye whiskey in America is made from a base of at least 51 percent rye grain along with other cereal grain.

SCOTCH WHISKY Scotch must be made in Scotland predominantly from malted barley, be bottled at least 80 proof, aged in oak barrels for a minimum of three years, and only water or caramel coloring can be added. Scotch can be divided in two major categories, the blends and the single malts. While blends can and do combine scotch whiskies from different grain bills and distilleries, single malts are strictly made from malted barley from the same distillery.

HIGHLAND SCOTCH Home to some of the most famous scotch brands in the world, Highland scotches tend to be spicy and oaky, with mild peat notes and a mild sweetness.

ISLAY SCOTCH Not for the faint of heart, Islay scotch is powerful and medicinally smoky with distinct peat flavors.

WINE

Wine as a category has so many different categories, styles, classifications, and caveats that it would be nigh on impossible to provide you with anything approaching useful information about wine that wouldn't fill another entire book. Instead, here are two pieces of advice. If you know what you like, drink it. If you don't know what you like, find a good wine bar or bottle shop, let them know what flavors you enjoy, and see if they have any recommendations. Wine people love wine and want you to enjoy it too!

Garnishes

While cocktail garnishes are essentially limited only by your own imagination, remember that they function almost like a playbill, hinting at the contents and ideally visually delightful. For example, let's take the classic Moscow Mule. With lime and ginger as its main flavor components, a lime wheel and a piece of candied ginger prime the palate for the drink to come. Often times, the garnish also enhances the aroma of the drink by expressing the oils of citrus peels over the top or along the rim. Sometimes the garnish is there simply as a nice little snack that adds flavor to the experience—a good briny olive in a martini, for example.

The following are some of the most commonly used garnishes and how to make them.

CANDIED GINGER

This chewy, sweet staple of many a mule-based cocktail can be purchased at just about any well-stocked grocery store that has a bulk foods section. I find I have to keep myself from eating them straight out of the package.

CITRUS

This is practically its own category, though for our purposes I've tried to break them into two basic sub-categories.

PEEL-ONLY This includes swaths, twists, and zest. To craft each, use the following guidelines:

SWATHS Confusingly named but virtually the simplest of all citrus garnishes. A swath is a piece of citrus peel usually cut from the stem end to the blossom end. For example, the "navel" on a navel orange. A good, sharp peeler will easily take nice wide swaths without getting a lot of the pit, though with a little practice, so will a paring knife. Once harvested from the fruit, you can trim or shape the swath however you like. For a "flame-cut" swath, for example, trim the swath into a thin four-sided diamond longer than it is wide, then make a thin slice running almost, but not quite, from tip to tip. This will create a notch that can be used to perch the garnish on the edge of a glass. Whenever a drink calls for a swath, squeeze the peel skin side down to express its oils onto the cocktail.

TWISTS: Thin long strips of peel from your citrus of choice. Treated with a little care, you can get twists to spiral like curling ribbon. They are super festive coiled around the straw of a long drink. If you picked up a Y peeler that has a little loop on the end (technically it's for the eyes on potatoes), then you're in business. Otherwise, either a channel knife or a lot of patience with your knife and peeler can result in long, beautiful strands of citrus peel. To get a nice tight spiral, I like to wrap the twist tightly around the handle of a barspoon or other thin tube, then slide it off and dress my cocktail.

ZEST: Finest of all citrus garnishes and mainly used for aroma. Specialty peelers called "zesters" are available but feel free to grab your microplane or the finest grater you have handy and gently scrape the zest from your washed citrus. Use immediately, as zest will dry out in mere minutes.

PEEL AND FLESH

WEDGES: The wedge is possibly the most commonly cut garnish in bars. Do it like the pros and make the first cut right through the stem and blossom ends. Then cut those halves into thirds. Perfect for placing on the rim of a cocktail. Note that with larger lemons or oranges, you may want to cut your wedges into eight pieces instead of six.

WHEELS: Wheels are great for when you want a relatively large garnish, but the drinker isn't likely to want to squeeze the garnish into the drink. Slice all the way through the fruit perpendicular to the stem end, creating "wheels" of citrus showing the individual segments. When cut very thin, these wheels can be perched on top of foamy cocktails or gently floated on a rim. Cut a bit thicker and with a notch in one side, they will easily perch on the edge of a glass.

COCKTAIL OLIVES

While the classic is the pimento olive—so named for the bit of mild red pepper (pimento) stuffed inside—next time that you're in the grocery store, look out for Castelvetrano olives. They are grown in Sicily and available stuffed with everything from chilis to garlic, pickles, and cheese. If your grocery store has an olive bar (usually near the cheese counter), make sure you're buying brine-packed olives. Save the oil-packed ones for salads and cheeseboards.

COCKTAIL ONIONS, AKA PICKLED PEARL ONIONS

While most often associated with the Gibson cocktail, a good-quality pickled onion can be a welcome addition to most any savory cocktail. This is where a Spanish-style gin and tonic gets a lovely vinegar punch, for example.

COCKTAIL CHERRIES

While a lemon is a lemon is a lemon, the same cannot be said of cocktail cherries. For too long, dessert cherries were sneaked into cocktails with varying levels of success. Thankfully, in the last decades or so, the cocktail cherry has been resurrected to its formerly exalted position as a pinnacle of sophisticated cocktails; adding in one or two can elevate an old-fashioned, Manhattan, or Tom Collins quite nicely.

CUCUMBER

Whether it's sliced thick as a wheel for muddling, perched on an herbaceous cocktail, or a superthin long slice off a peeler, cucumbers are light, bright, and refreshing. During the spring and summer, keep a few kicking around at all times.

SPICES AND SEASONINGS

While pre-ground spices can be tempting to buy due to the convenience factor, remember that they are likely ground too fine to be useful as garnish, and will have lost much of their aroma. A jar of nutmeg berries, a bag of cinnamon sticks, a tin of whole cloves, and both celery salt and coarse kosher salt should be useful for hundreds of different drinks and will last for a very long time. To use the whole spices, if you don't have a microplane or another very fine grater, you can scrape shavings onto your cocktail with your paring knife.

An American in Paris | *Evita*

SUNSET BLVD.

SOUTH PACIFIC

HOW TO SUCCEED IN BUSINESS WITHOUT REALLY TRYING

Les Misérables

JESUS CHRIST SUPERSTAR | BYE BYE BIRDIE

CHICAGO

Mamma Mia! | Oklahoma!

NUMBERS

LITTLE SHOP OF HORRORS | THE WHO'S TOMMY

The Sound of Music | THE WIZ

FUNNY GIRL | SINGIN' IN THE RAIN | ANNIE | KISS OF THE SPIDER WOMAN

GYPSY

Once on This Island | HELLO, DOLLY!

house in Texas

Cabaret

MUSIC BY
John Kander

BOOK BY
Joe Masteroff

LYRICS BY
Fred Ebb

BROADWAY OPENING
November 20, 1966
AT THE
Broadhurst Theatre

WEST END OPENING
February 28, 1968
AT THE
Palace Theatre

Fun Facts

The 1972 movie musical of *Cabaret* differs from the stage musical in significant ways. One of the biggest differences is that two main characters—Fräulein Schneider and Herr Schultz—are cut from the film, as are several songs that feature those characters, including "So What?" and "It Couldn't Please Me More (A Pineapple)."

NOMINATED TONYS
(ORIGINAL PRODUCTION)
10

WINNING TONYS
(ORIGINAL PRODUCTION)
8

Life Is a Cabernet

GLASS

chilled
wineglass

SERVES 1 *Willkommen!* Come hear the music play with this luscious red wine cocktail inspired by the 1966 Tony Award winner for Best Musical, *Cabaret*. Later gracing both the West End and the silver screen, *Cabaret* takes place within the confines of Berlin's seedy Kit Kat Klub in the 1930s, as the Nazi Party is rising to power. The heart of the show is cabaret singer Sally Bowles, whose unforgettable zest for life has been embodied by some of Hollywood's biggest names, including Judi Dench, Liza Minnelli, Natasha Richardson, and Michelle Williams. With iconic numbers such as "Mein Herr," "Money," and "Maybe This Time," the depth of this musical pairs perfectly with the depth of a rich Cabernet and blends well against the sweet and sour of a blend of fresh citrus. So, why sit alone in your room? Make yourself a cocktail and come to the cabaret.

4 oz. Cabernet or other medium-bodied dry red

½ oz. aged rum

1 tsp. of simple syrup

½ oz. lemon juice

½ oz. orange juice

Bartender's Note: This is a great choice for opening up a Tony-viewing cocktail party as it scales up to a punch quite nicely and instructions for just that are included as well.

Combine all ingredients in your shaker, add 5 to 6 ice cubes, seal, and shake hard until the tin is frosted over and the cubes have rounded edges. Strain onto fresh ice, garnish, and channel your best Liza.

GARNISH
depending on
your citrus
preference,
either a wheel
of lemon, lime,
or orange

1 750ml bottle of red wine

3 oz. of aged rum

4 barspoons of fine sugar

Juice of 1 whole lemon

Juice of 1 whole orange

PLAYING TO A CROWD? The following amounts will serve about a dozen guests and can be made up to two days prior to "opening night." It can also be doubled or tripled to no ill effect.

SERVES 12   Stir all ingredients together in a large bowl or sealable container until the sugar has dissolved, then chill in the fridge. When curtain call comes around, add a large block of ice to the punch bowl and garnish with fresh orange wheels.

West Side Story

MUSIC BY
Leonard
Bernstein

BOOK BY
Arthur
Laurents

LYRICS BY
Stephen
Sondheim

BROADWAY OPENING
September 26,
1957
AT THE
Winter Garden
Theatre

WEST END OPENING
December 12,
1958
AT THE
Her Majesty's
Theatre

Fun Facts

The cultural clash could have taken a very different turn: director and choreographer Jerome Robbins supposedly initially planned on pairing up a Jewish girl and an Italian Catholic boy on the Lower East Side of New York City.

NOMINATED TONYS
(ORIGINAL PRODUCTION)

6

WINNING TONYS
(ORIGINAL PRODUCTION)

2

West Sidecar Story

SERVES 1 *West Side Story* is known to dabble in a splash of conflict, as this classic highlights the war between rival street gangs in a tragedy of Shakespearean proportions, featuring the conflict between the Puerto Rican Sharks facing off against the white Jets.

Conflicts aside, *West Side Story* emerged as a real winner: Its film adaptation won ten Academy Awards, more than any other musical adaptation and a feat surpassed by only three other films: *The Return of the King*, *Titanic*, and *Ben-Hur*. That's an achievement worthy of a toast!

In our homage to this classic, two rival factions are at war with each other, engaged in a protracted conflict. The history of the sidecar is mired in conflict, with the "French school" insisting on equal parts cognac, Cointreau, and lemon juice, while the "English school" calls for a double dose of cognac.

Combine all ingredients in your shaker, add 5 to 6 ice cubes, seal, and shake hard until the tin is cold to the touch. Strain and garnish by expressing the orange peel over the glass then discarding it. Consume at a leisurely pace.

ENCORE
Flame the orange twist over the glass to add a slightly smoky aroma that will help tie the bourbon and cognac together.

GLASS

chilled coupe

---

1 oz. bourbon

1 oz. cognac

1 oz. Cointreau, Grand Marnier, or Combier

1 oz. fresh lemon juice

GARNISH
orange twist

Bye Bye Birdie

MUSIC BY
Charles
Strouse

BOOK BY
Michael
Stewart

LYRICS BY
Lee
Adams

BROADWAY OPENING
April 14, 1960
AT THE
Martin Beck
Theatre

WEST END OPENING
June 15, 1961
AT THE
Her Majesty's
Theatre

Fun Facts

Dick Van Dyke won his only Tony Award for his
lead role as Albert Peterson, a role that he reprised
for the 1963 film adaptation of the musical.

NOMINATED TONYS
(ORIGINAL PRODUCTION)
8

WINNING TONYS
(ORIGINAL PRODUCTION)
4

Fly High Birdie

double old-
fashioned or
your favorite
tiki mug

SERVES 1   Got a lot of livin' left to do? Then look no further than the tunes of 1960s Tony winner *Bye Bye Birdie*. Taking inspiration from the 1957 Army draft of Elvis Presley, this musical follows fictional teen heartthrob Conrad Birdie in his final concert before shipping out. Featuring legends Dick Van Dyke and Chita Rivera as Birdie's soon-to-be-unemployed manager, Albert, and his girlfriend, Rosie, in its Broadway debut, the musical went on to several revivals, a West End spinoff, and a film of the same name also starring Van Dyke as well as Janet Leigh in the lead roles. As you take in Birdie's Presley-esque hip twists and some upbeat '60s pop, enjoy the signature Fly High Birdie cocktail, a riff on the modern tiki classic Jungle Bird that makes good use of the complexity of Campari and a nice dark rum.

1½ oz. aged rum

¾ oz. Campari

¾ oz. honey simple syrup (can be shortened to ½ oz. if using a sweeter rum or if you simply prefer a drier cocktail)

Combine all ingredients in your shaker, add 5 to 6 ice cubes, seal, and shake hard until the tin is frosted over and the cubes have rounded edges. Strain onto fresh ice, garnish, and consume at speed.

1½ oz. fresh grapefruit juice (ruby red, ideally)

½ oz. fresh lime juice

ENCORE
Add a ¼ ounce of white rum for a totally different feel.

GARNISH
grapefruit twist

Honey Simple Syrup

SERVES 1 DRINK

Mix together equal parts honey and hot water, stirring thoroughly to combine. Allow to cool, then bottle. When chilled, it will keep pretty much indefinitely.

1 tbsp. honey

1 tbsp. hot water

Oliver!

MUSIC, BOOK, AND LYRICS BY
Lionel Bart

BROADWAY OPENING
January 6, 1963
AT THE
Imperial Theatre

WEST END OPENING
June 30, 1960
AT THE
New Theatre

Fun Facts

The film adaptation of *Oliver!* premiered in 1968 to widespread critical acclaim, and was nominated for eleven Academy Awards, winning six, including Best Picture.

NOMINATED TONYS
(ORIGINAL PRODUCTION)
9

WINNING TONYS
(ORIGINAL PRODUCTION)
3

GLASS

wineglass

1½ oz. carrot-
infused vodka
(see recipe
next page)

½ oz. tangelo
juice (navel
orange will do
just fine, but
please squeeze
your own!)

½ oz. lemon juice

½ oz. rosemary
simple syrup
(see recipe
next page)

½ oz. Picpoul de
Pinet (or any
such dry white
wine)

GARNISH
lemon wheel,
carrot ribbon

You've Got to Pick a Picpoul or Two

SERVES 1 Consider yourself at home and part of the family when viewing Lionel Bart's Tony- and Olivier-winning *Oliver!*, a musical adaptation of a lesser Dickens novel. Earning acclaim on both sides of the Atlantic following its 1960 West End premiere, the show is a perennial crowd-pleaser. With a diverse score that features showstoppers such as "Food, Glorious Food" and tearjerkers like "As Long as He Needs Me" and "Where Is Love?" and memorable characters like wily Fagin, the loveable Artful Dodger, and tragic Nancy, there's something in the show for every audience member.

And like the number that inspires its name, this brunchable, Instagram-friendly springtime stunner is a cocktail that you're sure to remember. It takes full advantage of bright citrus, woodsy rosemary, and the minerality of a dry white wine and is tasty enough to have you saying, "Please, sir, may I have some more?"

Combine all ingredients in your shaker, add 5 to 6 ice cubes, seal, and shake hard until the tin is frosted over. Strain onto cracked ice, then float the drink with a little seltzer. Place your garnish and drink in the sun, ideally on a picnic blanket with friends!

Carrot-Infused Vodka Two Ways

SERVES 5

SOUS VIDE METHOD
Set your water bath to 170 degrees. Combine the vodka and carrot in a zippered bag, being careful to remove as much air as possible from the bag prior to sealing. Place the bag in the water bath and set a timer for 40 minutes. Remove, then strain the solids out.

NO SOUS VIDE? NO PROBLEM.
Just steep the fresh carrot peels in the vodka in a sealed container for about four days, then strain. Will keep refrigerated for up to one month.

NOTE: If you don't have a peeler, grate the carrot over the coarse side of a grater, or cut into fine matchsticks if all you have is a knife. Using a peeler is a nice touch and you can reserve some for cocktail garnish.

1 cup of 80 proof (40 percent ABV) vodka

1 large carrot, peeled into ribbons

Rosemary Simple Syrup

MAKES 1 CUP

Combine in a small saucepan, bring to a boil, and let cook for one minute. Remove from heat, cover, and allow to cool. Strain out solids and store tightly sealed in the fridge.

NOTE: The infused vodka and herbal simple syrup can be made up to two weeks ahead of time.

1 cup water

1 cup white sugar

4 sprigs of rosemary

GLASS

chilled cocktail
glass or coupe

2½ oz. London
dry gin

½ oz. dry
vermouth

Optional: 1 or
2 dashes of
saline (see
note)

GARNISH
olive and
lemon twist

Oliver, er Twist

SERVES 1 Now that you consider yourself one of us, let's talk about martinis, mate. Specifically, two versions of the timeless tippler ending up in two very different drinks. The classic gin martini and its briny brother, the dirty martini. For starters, both of our tipples are going to end up being approximately 3 ounces of total ingredients. Sure, we may think we want a bigger cocktail, but martinis are best drunk quickly and as cold as possible. Sure, most cocktail glasses can hold a lot more, but the last third of your martini is likely to be too warm. Besides, if you find yourself saying, "Please, sir, may I have some more," just make another!

Start by chilling your glassware in the freezer. Into a mixing glass, combine the gin and vermouth over ice. Stir gently and quickly for no fewer than 30, but no more than 50, revolutions. Strain the finished cocktail into your now-chilled coupe or cocktail glass.

NOTE: Saline for bar use: 20 grams (just over 3 teaspoons) salt dissolved in 80 milliliters (a little less than 3 ounces) of water. Store in a glass dasher on the bar cart or drinks cabinet pretty much indefinitely.

The Dirty Oliver

SERVES 1 More of a Fagin or Artful Dodger–type? Then go for this naughtier version of the martini. Chill your cocktail glass or coupe as usual.

Combine ice, vodka, and olive brine in a shaker, seal with the other half of the shaker, and shake hard until the tin frosts slightly. Strain, serve, and enjoy.

GLASS

chilled coupe or cocktail glass

2½ oz. of vodka

½ oz. strained cocktail olive brine (Please avoid oil- or salt-packed olives for this recipe: They are lovely on the cheese plate but not suited to this drink.)

GARNISH
1 to 3 cocktail olives depending on whether the recipient is in need of a little food, glorious food

Jesus Christ Superstar

MUSIC BY
Andrew Lloyd Webber

LYRICS BY
Tim Rice

BROADWAY OPENING
October 12, 1971
AT THE
Mark Hellinger Theatre

WEST END OPENING
August 9, 1972
AT THE
Palace Theatre

NOMINATED TONYS (ORIGINAL PRODUCTION)
5

Fun Facts

Before it was produced for the stage, *Jesus Christ Superstar* was released in October 1970 as a concept rock opera album. It was a hit across the globe, and was even played by the Vatican's radio station.

GLASS

double old-
fashioned

1½ oz. gin

¾ oz. Campari

¾ oz. dry
vermouth

GARNISH
orange twist

I Don't Know How to Love Gin

SERVES 1   With music by Andrew Lloyd Webber and lyrics by Tim Rice, *Jesus Christ Superstar* is a show like no other. A rock opera that covers the last days in the life of Jesus of Nazareth, the show debuted on Broadway to critical acclaim in 1971 and has since spawned more than a dozen revivals and tours, two feature films, and a televised live concert version. With soaring vocal numbers and rock-and-roll-style guitar solos, the musical attracts a cultlike following of religious and nonreligious alike.

Everything's all right in this cocktail, which draws its name from Mary Magdalene's heartfelt ballad. Good day or night, this drink is a boozy sipper meant to whet the appetite and sooth a furrowed brow. Using dry vermouth and a Western-style gin, we get to explore the herbal side of Campari's bitter nature.

1 Combine all ingredients and 2 to 3 ice cubes in your mixing glass or build directly in a double old-fashioned if you need to (this is a great cocktail in an elevated hotel room), stir gently but rapidly with a barspoon, or a chopstick or pen or whatever if you're improvising. You're going to need to stir this longer than you think. We want the ice to melt a little bit to help the three components come together nicely.

2 You have a few different options for straining: Strain onto fresh ice in a double rocks glass, or as mentioned you can build the drink right in the glass you're going to drink from. Express your orange twist over the drink, drop it in. Sip, let the different flavors run across your tongue, feel a little bit of yourself stand just a bit easier.

How to Succeed in Business Without Really Trying

MUSIC AND LYRICS BY
Frank Loesser

BOOK BY
Abe Burrows, Jack Weinstock, and Willie Gilbert

BROADWAY OPENING
October 14, 1961
AT THE
46th Street Theatre

WEST END OPENING
March 28, 1963
AT THE
Shaftesbury Theatre

NOMINATED TONYS (ORIGINAL PRODUCTION) 8

WINNING TONYS (ORIGINAL PRODUCTION) 7

The Company Way with a (Lemon) Twist

SERVES 1 When J. Pierrepont Finch started working at World Wide Wicket Company, Mr. Twimble took the former window washer under his wing, and taught him that the secret to stability is doing everything "The Company Way"—of course, no true social climber could rise through the ranks by doing the Company Way, so Finch took that advice and gave it his own lemon twist at the end.

The Company Way with a (Lemon) Twist may start out as a humble Flannel Shirt featuring a scotch-whisky mix sure to satisfy palates from the mail room to the executive suite, with a touch of lemon juice and fruit to bring back fond memories of Grand Old Ivy. The truly adventurous can substitute Averna with Montenegro, but know that substituting amaros is risky business. And isn't it safer to do things the Company Way?

Stir—that's it. (I know what you're thinking: But it has juice in it! Rest easy, dear Broadway and cocktail buff, for there is method in our madness. We want smoothness and minimal aeration in our finished drink.) Combine all ingredients into your mixing glass, fill with ice, and stir with speed and vigor. After fifty turns, your drink is ready. Strain into your chilled glass, gently express the lemon twist over the top to release its oils, and if you're feeling fancy, perch the twist on the rim of the glass. Bring it to your nose, inhale deeply, then take a sip and enjoy.

GLASS

chilled Nick 'n' Nora or coupe

1¾ oz. scotch whisky

½ oz. single-malt whisky

½ oz. Averna

½ oz. lemon juice

3 dashes apple bitters

GARNISH
lemon twist

A Gentleman's Guide to Love and Murder

MUSIC BY
Steven Lutvak

BOOK AND LYRICS BY
Steven Lutvak and Robert L. Freedman

BROADWAY OPENING
November 17, 2013
AT THE
Walter Kerr Theatre

Fun Facts

Actor Jefferson Mays, who stayed with the show from its premiere on the Hartford Stage in October 2012 through its entire Broadway run, played the entire D'Ysquith family, an astounding nine roles. He won a Drama Desk Award and was nominated for a Tony for his efforts.

NOMINATED TONYS
(ORIGINAL PRODUCTION)

10

WINNING TONYS
(ORIGINAL PRODUCTION)

4

A Gentleman's Guide to Love and Margaritas

SERVES 1 Those of you of weaker constitution might want to take care when imbibing this recipe, as it has the potential to mix up enough margaritas to bring all the heirs of the second Earl of Highhurst down for the count.

Some people claim that the margarita can trace its origins to musical theatre: In the late 1930s, Ziegfeld Follies dancer Marjorie King was allergic to many spirits but could handle tequila. So, Carlos "Danny" Herrera mixed up the now-classic cocktail and named the drink after her—the "Margarita," Spanish for Margaret or Marjorie.

A Gentleman's Guide to Love and Murder protagonist Monty Navarro might not have been quite so considerate of King's allergy, as he left quite a body count behind him in pursuit of a mere earldom.

(Note that the ratio below means it's very easy to scale this recipe up for a crowd.)

Ratio: 4 Parts + 2 Parts + 2 Parts + 1 Part, where "a part" is ½ oz.

Combine all ingredients in a shaker tin, fill with ice, and shake hard until the tin is completely frosted over. Strain onto fresh ice in your rimmed double old-fashioned glass and enjoy.

NOTE: To rim, rub the outside edge of the glass with a cut lime wedge, then dip the now damp edge into a little salt on a small plate. Of course, if you have stemmed novelty margarita glasses, feel free to use them, but you may want to serve the drink neat lest the ice cubes put the drink in your lap.

Feel free to substitute with agave nectar if you prefer it. Also, if the resulting drink is a bit too sweet for your liking, cut the syrup to 1 teaspoon. The simple syrup will still affect the texture in pleasing ways, but the drink will be notably tarter.

GLASS

double old-fashioned rimmed halfway with coarse salt

---

2 oz. white tequila

1 oz. Cointreau (You can use Grand Marnier or even triple sec in a pinch, though you may find the resulting drink a bit too sweet.)

1 oz. fresh lime juice

½ oz. simple syrup

GARNISH
lime wedge or wheel

My Fair Lady

MUSIC BY
Frederick Loewe

BOOK AND LYRICS BY
Alan Jay Lerner

BROADWAY OPENING
March 15, 1956
AT THE
Mark Hellinger Theatre

WEST END OPENING
April 30, 1958
AT THE
Theatre Royal, Drury Lane

Fun Facts

Before the dynamic Broadway duo of Lerner and Loewe took a stab at adapting *Pygmalion* for the stage, Rodgers and Hammerstein tried and failed to get to the church on time.

NOMINATED TONYS
(ORIGINAL PRODUCTION)
10

WINNING TONYS
(ORIGINAL PRODUCTION)
6

GLASS

chilled coupe

---

4 to 5 fresh
raspberries
and 1 for
garnish

½ oz. simple
syrup

Optional: 1 dash
bitters

¾ oz. lemon juice

2 oz. vodka (or a
stiff London gin
if you prefer)

The Royal Ascot

SERVES 1   Wouldn't it be loverly to class it up a bit? Then it's time to look toward Lerner and Loewe's 1956 masterpiece, *My Fair Lady*. A twist on the Greek Pygmalion myth, in this version uptight Professor Henry Higgins bets a friend that he can pass off a Cockney flower seller as a lady. It's earned its way into the pantheon of Broadway staples, spurring dozens of revivals and an Oscar-winning film adaptation.

If you're looking to have your own *My Fair Lady*–like transformation, this cocktail will have you feeling classy in no time, with its charming pale blush color, inspired by Ms. Doolittle's signature dress for the Royal Ascot. From there it would have been simple enough to channel our best Cockney and christen this "Pink Drink!," but you deserve better. As such, our theatrics-loving bartender has incorporated some of the classic flavors of a day at the races to bring you a Royal Ascot. This recipe can be doubled in a single shaker tin should you have a little bit of luck to be drinking with a fellow musical lover.

In a mixing tin, combine the raspberries, simple syrup, and bitters. Muddle the mixture just until you smell the raspberries. Remove the muddler (or a wooden spoon or sanitized end of a dowel or what have you). Add the lemon juice, then the vodka, and fill the shaker with ice. Now hard shake the mixture to chill and aerate. Fine strain into your coupe, drop in the remaining fresh raspberry, and drink swiftly.

The Rain in Spain

SERVES 1   Because the soundtrack of *My Fair Lady*—especially if you're listening to the original Broadway cast with the incomparable Dame Julie Andrews as Eliza and the ever-stalwart Rex Harrison as Professor Higgins—will have you dancing all night and begging for more, a second cocktail for this musical is in order. This scrumptious concoction won't be staying mainly in the plain, as it combines a reduced-proof Iberian variation of a French 75, and then the fruit-forward flavors of rosé cava, citrusy Spanish-style gin, and fresh produce to produce a fantastic brunch, afternoon aperitive, or after-dinner cocktail. Take care when imbibing if you need to get to the church on time, as this one packs a punch!

In a shaker tin combine the lemon juice, simple syrup, bitters, and strawberries. Muddle the strawberries thoroughly, then add the gin and Pimm's. Add ice, give it a good hard shake to chill, and then fine strain into the champagne flute or coupe. Float cava gently into the glass to finish, and perch on the rim or drop the remaining strawberry slice in the drink. Just don't let the finished drink fall upon the plain!

NOTE: If you can, try to get these types of gin for an authentic taste: Mahon, Sipsmith Lemon, Tanqueray Malacca, or Watershed Four Peel.

GLASS

champagne flute or large coupe

¼ oz. fresh lemon juice

¼ oz. simple syrup

1 dash bitters

2 fresh strawberries and 1 slice of strawberry cut from tip to stem

½ oz. Spanish-style gin

¼ oz. Pimm's Cup No. 1

Sparkling rosé cava to fill

A Little Night Music

MUSIC AND LYRICS BY
Stephen Sondheim

BOOK BY
Hugh Wheeler

BROADWAY OPENING
February 25, 1973
AT THE
Shubert Theatre

WEST END OPENING
April 15, 1975
AT THE
Adelphi Theatre

Fun Facts

The show is a vocal challenge for nearly the entire cast, as the music and lyrics of the work are written in a style more often seen in operetta or light opera. The show makes use of counterpoint, contrapuntal duets and trios, and other complex musical styles. As such, it has been performed by several different opera companies, including a successful run with the New York City Opera company in 1990.

NOMINATED TONYS
(ORIGINAL PRODUCTION)
12

WINNING TONYS
(ORIGINAL PRODUCTION)
6

A Little Night Cap

SERVES 1   Take a little waltz with us before we send in the clowns after our eleven o'clock number. Set in Sweden at the turn of the century, Sondheim's classic *A Little Night Music* follows the romantic life of actress Desiree Armfeldt and those in her circle. Winning the Tony for Best Musical in 1973, *A Little Night Music* garnered acclaim across the pond as well and was produced for the big screen, with a star-studded cast, including Elizabeth Taylor, Diana Rigg, Len Cariou, and Lesley-Anne Down. Although the score is known to be a vocal challenge for its actors, our Little Night Cap is sure to go down smooth, as it's sweet but not cloying, herbaceous, and slightly minty. Supposedly Victoria Mallory was said to enjoy one every night after the evening performance of *A Little Night Music* at the Shubert Theatre during its original Broadway run.

Combine the vermouth and gin in a mixing glass over ice. Stir thoroughly to combine, then strain into the Nick 'n' Nora or coupe. Finally, pour the Fernet over the back of a spoon placed just above the drink's surface to create a layered effect. If using, express the lemon twist over the glass, then discard.

GLASS

chilled Nick 'n' Nora or small coupe

¾ oz. sweet Italian vermouth

1½ oz. London dry gin

½ oz. Fernet-Branca

GARNISH
expressed lemon twist (optional)

Mary Poppins

MUSIC BY
Richard M. Sherman,
Robert B. Sherman,
and George Stiles

LYRICS BY
Richard M. Sherman,
Robert B. Sherman,
and Anthony Drewe

BOOK BY
Julian Fellowes

BROADWAY OPENING
November 16,
2006
AT THE
New
Amsterdam
Theatre

WEST END OPENING
December 15,
2004
AT THE
Prince
Edward
Theatre

NOMINATED TONYS
(ORIGINAL PRODUCTION)

7

WINNING TONYS
(ORIGINAL PRODUCTION)

1

Martini Poppins

SERVES 1 Walt Disney's take on P. L. Travers's beloved nanny finally made its way to the West End and Great White Way in 2004 and 2006, respectively. With a book by *Downton Abbey* creator Julian Fellowes, the score features many of the Sherman Brothers' toe-tapping numbers like "Step in Time" and "Chim Chim Cher-ee" and classics like "Supercalifragilisticexpialidocious" and "Let's Go Fly a Kite." *Mary Poppins* is beloved by kids of all ages. And if you're a kid over the age of twenty-one, we recommend taking a jolly holiday with our Martini Poppins. Our "practically perfect" martini variation would be fit for Mary herself, though it's a bit drier and boozier than her typical cordials. Definitely beats a spoonful of sugar at any rate.

Combine all ingredients in a mixing glass, add ice, and stir thoroughly to chill and dilute. Strain and garnish by expressing, then dropping, the twist into the cocktail.

GLASS

chilled coupe

---

2 oz. dry gin

½ oz. dry vermouth

½ oz. sweet vermouth

GARNISH
lemon or orange twist

Kiss of the Spider Woman

MUSIC BY
John Kander

BOOK BY
Terrence McNally

LYRICS BY
Fred Ebb

BROADWAY OPENING
May 3, 1993
AT THE
Broadhurst Theatre

WEST END OPENING
October 20, 1992
AT THE
Shaftesbury Theatre

Fun Facts

Despite its very dark themes, *Kiss of the Spider Woman* is featured heavily in an episode of the teen drama *Katy Keene*, where the show is put on by several characters.

NOMINATED TONYS
(ORIGINAL PRODUCTION)
11

WINNING TONYS
(ORIGINAL PRODUCTION)
7

Kiss of the Spider Whiskey

GLASS

double old-
fashioned

SERVES 1 While some musicals are all mirth and melodies, others delve into the darker side of the human spirit; *Kiss of the Spider Woman* falls solidly into that latter category. Based on Argentinian writer Manuel Puig's novel of the same name, the story toggles between the fantasies and realities of Luis Alberto Molina, an imprisoned gay man. Opening on the West End in 1992 and coming to Broadway in 1993, mixed reviews didn't stop *Kiss of the Spider Woman* from winning seven Tony Awards, including Best Musical, Best Director for Broadway baron Harold Prince, and Best Actress for leading lady Chita Rivera.

This deadly concoction takes its primary inspiration from the unofficial liquor of its namesake's setting. Oddly enough, Argentina's most popular spirit is an Italian amaro called Fernet-Branca. While usually consumed *con coca*, the below cocktail is decidedly stiffer and American, and should be handled with caution. It can be as deadly as the Spider Woman's Kiss.

1 oz. Fernet-Branca

1 oz. overproof bourbon

¾ oz. fresh lemon juice

¾ oz. simple syrup

GARNISH
fat lemon
wedge, mint
sprig

Combine all ingredients in your shaker tin. Add ice, and shake hard to chill and dilute. Strain into your glass over cracked ice if you're feeling fancy, or just use regular cubes if in a hurry. Enjoy how the menthol of the Fernet cools the bourbon burn, while the lemon and mint garnish highlights the aromatics.

Fiddler on the Roof

MUSIC BY
Jerry Bock

BOOK BY
Joseph Stein

LYRICS BY
Sheldon Harnick

BROADWAY OPENING
September 22, 1964
AT THE
Imperial Theatre

WEST END OPENING
February 16, 1967
AT THE
Her Majesty's Theatre

Fun Facts

Leading lady Bette Midler was part of the original Broadway cast, playing Tzeitel in 1966.

NOMINATED TONYS
(ORIGINAL PRODUCTION)
10

WINNING TONYS
(ORIGINAL PRODUCTION)
9

GLASS

chilled Nick 'n'
Nora or small
coupe

---

2 oz. rye whiskey

1 oz. Amaro
Bràulio

2–3 dashes of
Angostura
bitters

1–2 dashes of
Regan's orange
bitters

GARNISH
another
cocktail cherry
or an orange
twist

If I Were a Rich Man(hattan)

SERVES 1 Based on a series of intertwined Yiddish stories, the iconic *Fiddler on the Roof* centers on poor milkman Tevye, living in a Russian shtetl at the turn of the century, as he attempts to marry off his five daughters. Taking home nine Tony awards, including Best Musical, the original 1964 production ran for an impressive ten years, making it the longest-running musical at the time. *Fiddler* has made a match in the hearts of theatregoers everywhere, having spawned no less than five Broadway revivals in the subsequent years, an acclaimed West End run in 1967, and a classic 1971 musical film that was nominated for eight Academy Awards.

This velvety variant on New York City's most famous libation will have you strutting like a peacock and shouting "L'chaim." We will be substituting the usual sweet vermouth for a robust alpine amaro to create a fuller, "richer" experience. Take it easy with this potent concoction as it could cross a rabbi's eyes.

Combine all ingredients in a mixing glass and add ice. Stir thoroughly to combine, chill, dilute, then strain into the Nick 'n' Nora or coupe. Add your cocktail cherry or express the orange twist over the glass, then drop into the drink.

NOTE: If you can't find Bràulio, Amaro dell'Etna is a great substitute, or if in a real pinch, Jägermeister, though then reduce to ¾ oz.

South Pacific

MUSIC BY
Richard Rodgers

LYRICS BY
Oscar Hammerstein II

BOOK BY
Oscar Hammerstein II and Joshua Logan

BROADWAY OPENING
April 7, 1949
AT THE
Majestic Theatre

WEST END OPENING
November 1, 1951
AT THE
Theatre Royal, Drury Lane

Fun Facts

The song "Some Enchanted Evening" was the number one song in the United States in 1949, and was peformed by some of the nation's biggest crooners, including Frank Sinatra, Perry Como, and Bing Crosby.

NOMINATED TONYS
(ORIGINAL PRODUCTION)
10

WINNING TONYS
(ORIGINAL PRODUCTION)
10

GLASS

collins or your
favorite tropical
glass

---

2 oz. vodka
(bonus points
if you can find
a Hawaiian
brand)

1 oz. lime juice

2 oz. pineapple
juice

1 oz. blue curaçao

Soda water to
float

GARNISH
pineapple
wedge or lime
wheel

The South Pacific Breeze

SERVES 1 Building on America's post–World War II patriotic fervor, Rodgers and Hammerstein's fourth collaborative effort was based on several of the stories in James A. Michener's Pulitzer Prize–winning collection, *Tales of the South Pacific*. The show's original 1949 Broadway 1,925-performance run opened in the iconic Majestic Theatre to rave reviews and went on to snag a whopping ten Tony awards, including Best Musical. To date, the original run holds the distinction of being the only musical to take home the prize for all four acting categories: Best Actor in a Musical, Best Actress in a Musical, Best Featured Actor in a Musical, and Best Featured Actress in a Musical. And if that's not reason enough to celebrate with a tropical cocktail, we don't know what is!

Just as there's nothing like a dame, there's nothing quite like our twist on the Pacific Breeze. From the volcanic slopes of Kauai, this less-sweet cousin of the Blue Hawaiian creates a tropical sipper equally at home poolside as it is rooftop, and it pairs well with the cast recordings of any of *South Pacific*'s storied runs.

Combine all ingredients except soda in your shaker tin. Add ice and shake to chill. Strain onto crushed ice if at all possible, then float with a splash of soda water. Garnish, stick a fun straw into the middle, and take a trip to Bali Ha'i.

The Oscar Hammered-Stein (or Some En-Shandy-ed Evening)

GLASS

chilled pint glass

SERVES 1   Although its original run closed in 1954, *South Pacific*'s enchanting score and strong stance against racism have long stood the test of time, spurring several revivals over the ensuing decades, a 1958 feature film, and a handful of television adaptations. A number of the Great White Way's leading dames have taken on the scrubs of spunky but naïve Navy nurse Nellie Forbush, including Mary Martin, Florence Henderson, Kelli O'Hara, Laura Osnes, and Reba McEntire.

Listening to the timeless score that includes classics like "Bali Ha'i," "I'm Gonna Wash That Man Right Outta My Hair," and "Some Enchanted Evening" calls for a suitably light and timeless libation, such as our take on the summer shandy. When a steamy city summer has sapped your spirit, look no further than this high-test version of a classic cooler. While our variation calls for a stiff pour of vodka to be added to the mix, a perfectly lovely shandy can be had by omitting the spirits.

4 oz. lemonade (There is a recipe below if you're inclined to make it from scratch.)

2 oz. citrus vodka (optional, though awfully fun)

10 oz. Helles-style lager

Pour the lemonade and vodka directly into the pint glass, then angle the glass to the side while pouring the beer in so as to keep as much of the fizz as possible while still causing the ingredients to mix. Top with a lemon wedge perched on the edge and enjoy.

GARNISH
lemon wedge

Lemonade

MAKES APPROXIMATELY 1 QUART OR ENOUGH FOR 8 "BEERTAILS"

Combine all ingredients and stir thoroughly. The finished recipe will keep covered in the fridge for up to five days.

1 cup simple syrup

1 cup fresh lemon juice

2 cups water (if the resulting mixture is too intense, add a half cup of water)

Hello, Dolly!

MUSIC AND LYRICS BY
Jerry Herman

BOOK BY
Michael Stewart

BROADWAY OPENING
January 16, 1964
AT THE
St. James Theatre

WEST END OPENING
December 2, 1965
AT THE
Theatre Royal, Drury Lane

Fun Facts

The iconic red sequin dress worn by Carol Channing
in the Broadway premiere of the show is part of
a permanent display at the National Museum of
American History in Washington, DC.

NOMINATED TONYS
(ORIGINAL PRODUCTION)
11

WINNING TONYS
(ORIGINAL PRODUCTION)
10

GLASS

chilled coupe

1½ oz. white rum

¾ oz. lime juice

¼ oz. grapefruit juice

¾ oz. simple syrup

½ oz. Peychaud's Aperitivo (reserved)

Hello, Daiquiri!

SERVES 1 There are few Broadway leading ladies as strong-willed and as strong-minded as matchmaker Dolly Gallagher Levi. Challenged with the task of finding a wife for half-a-millionaire business owner Horace Vandergelder, the title heroine employs charm, cunning, and a zest for life to secure him a match. Played by Carol Channing in the original Broadway run, a laundry list's worth of grand dames such as Pearl Bailey, Phyllis Diller, Barbra Streisand, Ethel Merman, Betty Grable, Ginger Rogers, Bernadette Peters, and Bette Midler have all known that it takes a woman to fill Dolly's storied shoes.

And a character as iconic and memorable as Dolly deserves an equally bold cocktail, one that's got elegance. Luckily our vivacious take on the daiquiri is up to the task. To concoct one worthy of Dolly herself will take a few tweaks and a finishing touch of bright red Peychaud's Aperitivo to add complexity and a lovely red head.

Combine all ingredients except the Peychaud's in your shaker tin. Add 4 to 5 ice cubes and shake hard to chill, dilute, and aerate the cocktail. Fine strain, if possible, to remove any chips of ice into the chilled coupe. Carefully layer the Peychaud's on top of the cocktail by pouring it slowly over the back of a spoon hovering just above the surface of the drink.

Bloody Bloody Andrew Jackson

MUSIC AND LYRICS BY
Michael Friedman

BOOK BY
Alex Timbers

NOMINATED TONYS (ORIGINAL PRODUCTION)

2

BROADWAY OPENING
September 21, 2010
AT THE
Bernard B. Jacobs Theatre

Fun Facts

With an emo rock concert–style feel and told in a comedic manner, *Bloody Bloody Andrew Jackson* drew decidedly mixed reviews from audiences and critics, and ran for only 120 performances. It drew especially harsh criticism from Native American communities for its depictions of Indigenous communities.

GLASS

12-ounce collins
or tumbler

½ lemon divided
in two wedges

Enough celery
salt on a plate or
cutting board to
rim your glass

¾ tsp.
Worcestershire
sauce

¼ tsp. soy sauce
(low sodium
ideally)

¾ tsp. Old Bay
Seasoning

¼ tsp. hot sauce

½ tsp. freshly
grated
horseradish
or double
that amount
of prepared
horseradish

4 oz. good tomato
juice

2 oz. vodka,
London gin,
or tequila
(respectively
the Bloody
Mary, Bloody
Caesar, or
Bloody Maria)

Bloody Bloody Mary Jackson

SERVES 1   When Andrew Jackson was sworn into office in 1829 as America's first populist president, Senator James Hamilton of South Carolina described the inaugural festivities as a "regular Saturnalia," and alledgely Jackson's steward had to lure the crowd of revelers out of the White House with large tubs of whiskey punch. And while this savory take on the Bloody Mary may not include whiskey, the spices still pack a punch worthy of paying respects to *Bloody Bloody Andrew Jackson*.

While Alexander Hamilton's musical send-up embraced rap as its medium, *Bloody Bloody Andrew Jackson* turned to punk rock to document Old Hickory's populist rise and blood-soaked history. This savory concoction is the perfect tip of the hat to the musical since it's a drink as American as they come. Oh sure, the French may think they have a claim to the drink since Fernand Petiot first came up with the idea of mixing tomato juice and vodka while he was working at Harry's New York Bar in Paris. But Petiot didn't add the drink's transformative spice mixture until he brought it to the United States. We'll take the drink back from the French, and other countries too. I'm pretty sure it's our drink, anyway.

For an encore presentation, the Bloody Bloody Mary Jackson can scale up to serve a crowd of ten—not quite enough to fill a tub, but enough to make your guests say "Yea Yea!"

This super-savory version brings extra umami to the party with the addition of soy sauce, Old Bay Seasoning, and a generous rim of celery salt. This recipe can be made ahead for a crowd by simply multiplying each measure by the number of bloodies you plan to serve and in your bartender's opinion is much better after about three days in the fridge. (Details on the next page.)

While the recipe on the next page calls for the classic celery stalk and lemon wedge garnish, feel free to go off script with your garnish fun. (Our trusty bartender's favorite bloody garnish involves house-made pickles, a cherry tomato, and a cheese cube, but indulge your creative license. If it would work on a charcuterie or crudité board, it probably works in a bloody.)

Rim the glass in celery salt by running the edge of one of the lemon quarters along the side, then dipping the glass into the celery salt. Squeeze one of the lemon quarters into your mixing tin and discard the spent fruit. Combine the rest of the ingredients, add ice, then carefully pour the mixture back and forth into a large enough vessel. (This is called "rolling" a drink, and a 1-cup measuring glass works great.) Pour into your rimmed glass, garnish, and enjoy.

GARNISH
celery salt,
lemon wedge,
and celery stalk

NOTE: If you don't have Old Bay, substitute fresh ground black pepper, a pinch of cayenne, and a dash of mustard. Try to avoid "from concentrate" stuff; it always tastes a little metallic.

ENCORE
This recipe makes a wonderful batched mix for a brunch crowd of ten, or just a ready-made eye-opener should you need it.

1 Combine all ingredients. Stir to combine, then keep refrigerated in a sealed container for up to two weeks.

2 To make a cocktail, measure 6½ ounces of the ready-made batch, then add your lemon juice and booze of choice.

2½ tbsp. Worcestershire sauce

2½ tbsp. Old Bay Seasoning

2½ tsp. soy sauce

2½ tsp. hot sauce

5 tsp. freshly grated horseradish

5 cups fresh tomato juice

20 oz. vodka, London gin, or tequilla

Beauty and the Beast

MUSIC BY
Alan Menken

BOOK BY
Linda Woolverton

LYRICS BY
Howard Ashman and Tim Rice

BROADWAY OPENING
April 18, 1994
AT THE
Palace Theatre

WEST END OPENING
April 29, 1997
AT THE
Dominion Theatre

NOMINATED TONYS
(ORIGINAL PRODUCTION)
9

WINNING TONYS
(ORIGINAL PRODUCTION)
1

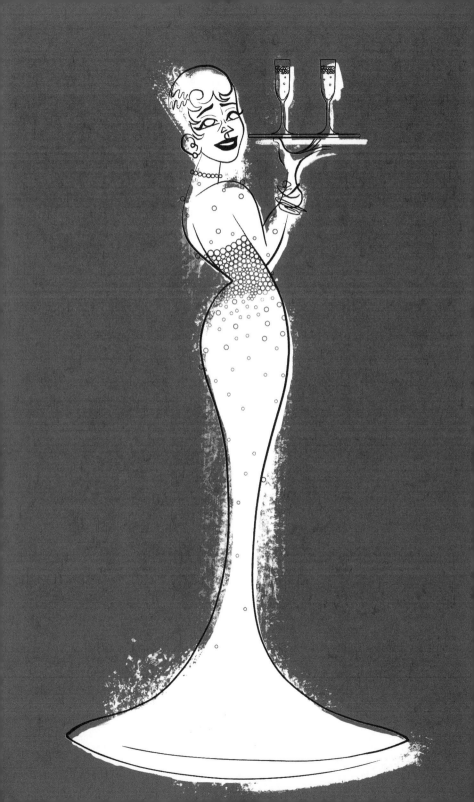

GLASS

chilled
champagne
flute or coupe

½ oz. peach
liqueur

1 to 2 drops of
orange flower
water

4 to 5 oz. of any
dry sparkling
white wine
(Prosecco
being the go-to)

GARNISH
peach slice,
if in season

Beauty and the Bellini

SERVES 1   It's a tale as old as time, one that's as sure as the sun rising in the east: bold and brave girl tames the monster to redeem the man inside. Based on the Academy Award–winning animated Disney movie of the same name, *Beauty and the Beast* opened on the Broadway stage in 1994, with Broadway pros Susan Egan and Terrence Mann in the titular roles. The show enchanted audiences of all ages for thirteen years and 5,461 performances, becoming the tenth longest-running show in Broadway history.

  This iteration of an all-time brunch classic pairs a neater presentation with a French Riviera twist. Our version forgoes the traditional, if messy, peach puree in favor of a peach liqueur and a few drops of orange flower water. Best served at brunch, lunch, or as an aperitivo in the late afternoon when asking friends and family to be your guest.

Add the peach liqueur and drop of orange flower water to the glass, top with sparkling wine. Garnish if you so choose.

The Who's Tommy

MUSIC AND LYRICS BY
Pete Townshend

BOOK BY
Pete Townshend and Des McAnuff

BROADWAY OPENING
April 22, 1993
AT THE
St. James Theatre

WEST END OPENING
March 5, 1996
AT THE
Shaftesbury Theatre

Fun Facts

The stage show is based on the Who's 1969 rock opera concept album of the same name and was made into a feature-length film in 1975.

NOMINATED TONYS
(ORIGINAL PRODUCTION)
11

WINNING TONYS
(ORIGINAL PRODUCTION)
5

The Who's Tommy Collins

GLASS

collins

---

2 oz. dry London gin

¾ oz. rhubarb juice (see next page)

¾ oz. simple syrup

Seltzer to fill

GARNISH
split rhubarb stalk

SERVES 1 In May 1874, the *St. Louis Post-Dispatch* reported on a practical joke that would soon become known as "The Great Tom Collins Hoax of 1874." According to the *Dispatch*, pranksters would approach a friend and ask, "Have you seen Tom Collins?" The bewildered victim would respond, "No. Who the deuce is Tom Collins?" The prankster would inform the man that Tom Collins was out there spreading horrible rumors and lies about the victim, and direct the man to a bar or saloon filled with confederates eager to lead the poor mark on a wild-goose chase in pursuit of the nefarious and purely fictional Tom Collins. Some claim that this hoax is what gave the Tom Collins its name, as bartenders started interpreting requests for Tom Collins as a drink order. Given the drink's storied history, "Who's Tommy Collins?" is a demand that likely echoed out in bars and saloons in the earliest days of the drink's existence.

The Who's classic rock musical *Tommy* followed the life of Pinball Wizard Tommy from his birth and early childhood in London during World War II. As an homage to *Tommy*'s wartime roots, this Tom Collins variant omits citrus, which was difficult to obtain in Britain due to rationing. As luck would have it, the intensely tart rhubarb was homegrown and readily available, making it the perfect substitution. While it's more work to extract rhubarb juice, its unique flavor is a welcome addition to this beautiful cocktail. But if rhubarb juice is as hard to come by as citrus was during rationing, an alternative recipe makes a serviceable substitute using lemon juice.

The Who's Tommy Collins might not be a miracle cure to all that ails you, but it's guaranteed to be a sensation at your next event, bringing out your inner Pinball Wizard. In this variant, we will pay homage to the wartime English setting in which The Who's *Tommy* begins.

Combine the gin, rhubarb juice, and simple syrup right in the glass using a barspoon, swizzle, or a straw; stir the mixture to incorporate the juice and simple syrup. Next add a few ice cubes and the split rhubarb stalk. Fill the glass with seltzer, stir a little, and serve!

Variations to Rhubarb Juice

SERVES 1 While there are at least four different techniques for juicing rhubarb at home, without knowing what gear is available to you, I'll instead direct you to look up "rhubarb juice recipe" via the search engine of your choosing.

1 As an alternative that will produce a lovely, if not quite as visually striking, cocktail, use the listed ingredients with the same instructions as above.

2 Garnish with a lemon wheel and a cocktail cherry.

2 oz. gin

¾ oz. lemon juice

½ oz. simple syrup

¼ oz. cocktail cherry syrup, pomegranate molasses, or grenadine

Seltzer to fill

Cats

MUSIC BY
Andrew Lloyd Webber

LYRICS BY
T. S. Eliot, Trevor Nunn, and Richard Stilgoe

BROADWAY OPENING
October 7, 1982
AT THE
Winter Garden Theatre

WEST END OPENING
May 11, 1981
AT THE
New London Theatre

Fun Facts

Madame Tussauds New York features several wax figurines of various *Cats* characters, including a full-size Grizabella that sings several bars of "Memory" for the museum's visitors.

NOMINATED TONYS
(ORIGINAL PRODUCTION)

11

WINNING TONYS
(ORIGINAL PRODUCTION)

7

Rum Tum Tugger

highball or
collins

SERVES 1   A posse of diverse Jellicle cats come together one night to decide—via musical interludes—who will ascend to a better life. Despite its rather odd premise, since its debut in 1981, Andrew Lloyd Webber's *Cats* has become one of the most recognizable musicals ever to grace the stage. Based on poet T. S. Eliot's *Old Possum's Book of Practical Cats*, anyone who has ever seen the show will have a distinct "memory" of its prancing felines, mesmerizing dance numbers, and colorful characters. Like its namesake feline, this cocktail stands out of the crowd. A distant cousin of a Gainsbourg Daisy cocktail, it is oddly tropical despite the only bit of it hailing from the tropics being the rum. The Chartreuse elevates the rum, while the Amaretto gives the drink legs for days (and might give you nine lives).

Combine all ingredients in your shaker, add 5 to 6 ice cubes, seal, and give a firm but brief shake. Strain onto crushed ice (or cracked, so long as they aren't just plain cubes). Stick a straw (reusable, please) down through the ice, set your lime wheel at a jaunty angle, and try to avoid brain freeze.

¾ oz. of dark rum

½ oz. green Chartreuse (or a fifty-fifty mix of St-Germain and Pernod)

¼ oz. Amaretto

1 oz. fresh lime juice

¾ oz. orange juice

GARNISH
lime wheel

The Jelly-cul Choice

SERVES 1   While this tasty winter warmer may not send you to the Heaviside Layer, the drink and its creative method will unlock a whole new range of fun choices either on the road or at home. When you find yourself trying to fashion a cocktail out of mixers you can get from a continental breakfast spread or airport restaurant, don't despair: you can use jelly (or maple syrup) to essentially make a rich simple syrup that packs a ton of flavor and a pleasant mouthfeel into a tidy package. If the base spirit changes, simply swap out the available jelly. Use the key at the bottom of the recipe for your particular booze.

GLASS

warmed mug ideally, but a disposable coffee cup from your in-room coffee service will work great in a pinch.

Fresh water

½ oz. (1 tbsp.) apple jelly

1½ oz. apple brandy

¾ oz. lemon juice (about 3 to 4 lemon wedges' worth)

¼ oz. St. Elizabeth Allspice Dram

GARNISH
lemon or orange twist (optional)

Fill the coffee maker or kettle with fresh water and turn it on. Make sure you have two cups handy, since you will need to swap them at one point if using the typical individual-portion coffee maker. Empty the jelly packet into your cup, then place it under the spout. As soon as the hot water begins filling the cup, let 1½ to 2 ounces into the cup, then swap it out. Stir the jelly and hot water together to fully dissolve the preserves. Add the remaining ingredients, then top with more hot water. Garnish by expressing then dropping the twist into the cocktail. Sip your toddy and resolve never to settle for minibar booze and whatever you can get from the vending machine next to the ice maker again.

NOTE: No Allspice Dram? No problem. A dash of Angostura bitters will add a nice complexity and dryness to the finished toddy.

YOU HAVE	TRY
Vodka	Strawberry, grape, mixed fruit, marmalade
Gin	Strawberry, grape, marmalade, apple
Rum	Mixed fruit, marmalade, apple, maple
Whiskey	Mixed fruit, marmalade, apple, maple
Tequila	Marmalade, apple, lemon, maple
Brandy	Apple, marmalade

The Best Little Whorehouse in Texas

MUSIC AND LYRICS BY
Carol Hall

BOOK BY
Larry L. King and
Peter Masterson

BROADWAY OPENING
June 19,
1978
AT THE
46th Street
Theatre

WEST END OPENING
February 26,
1981
AT THE
Theatre Royal,
Drury Lane

NOMINATED TONYS
(ORIGINAL PRODUCTION)
7

WINNING TONYS
(ORIGINAL PRODUCTION)
2

The Best Little Whiskey Sour in Texas

GLASS

double old-fashioned, prepped as described below

---

1 mesquite chip, food-grade only

2 oz. bourbon

¾ oz. lemon juice

¾ oz. honey simple syrup

1 egg white

GARNISH
lemon twist

SERVES 1   There's no drinking allowed at *The Best Little Whorehouse in Texas*'s Chicken Ranch brothel, so you'll have to look farther afield to find a stiff drink—you might even find yourself having to go seventy-five miles or more to find this smoky variation on an old-school whiskey sour. The Best Little Whiskey Sour in Texas is the perfect drink for of-age Aggie footballers to celebrate their win without getting the proprietress of a lil' ole bitty pissant country place in trouble with the law.

When Dolly Parton took on the lead role of Mona Stangley for the film adaptation of this 1978 musical, she brought one of her own hit songs to the production—the classic country love ballad "I Will Always Love You." The song had already topped Billboard's Hot Country Songs charts once in 1974, and her 1982 rerecording helped the song take the number one spot a second time . . . before Whitney Houston's cover of the song for *The Bodyguard* made history as the best-selling physical single by a woman in music history. That's something to make any good old girl smile.

Ol' Ed Earl Dodd himself would love this smoky variation on an old-school-style whiskey sour. Perfect for savoring while the Melvin P. Thorpe singers carry on about copulation and corruption.

Before you start the cocktail, let's smoke the glassware. On a solid fireproof surface (a ceramic plate, brick, etc.), light the mesquite chip on fire, then cover with the double old-fashioned glass. The fire will snuff immediately, and the wood chip will begin to fill the glass with woodsmoke. If using a wooden strike-anywhere match, allow the tip to burn off completely before covering, or the glass will have a sulfurous chemical odor. Our bartender loves using a culinary torch, but with a little patience a lighter will do the job.

Method continues

In a shaker tin, combine all ingredients, add ice, then tightly seal with the other half of the shaker. Shake hard to chill and integrate the mixture. Next open the tin, then strain the contents from the large side of the tin to the smaller and discard the ice. Now reseal the tins and shake vigorously for about ten seconds. Flip over the double old-fashioned glass with a flourish, add either one jumbo ice cube if available, or four or so ice tray–size cubes, then pour the foamy cocktail on top. Express the oil from your lemon twist onto the foam, then rest the twist on the drink.

NOTE: Mesquite chips are available at most hardware stores, online, or in many big-box retailers near the grills and patio bric-a-brac. A wooden match will work in a pinch if you can't lay hands on food-grade wood chips.

Rent

MUSIC, BOOK, AND LYRICS BY
Jonathan Larson

BROADWAY OPENING
April 29, 1996
AT THE
Nederlander Theatre

WEST END OPENING
May 12, 1998
AT THE
Shaftesbury Theatre

Fun Facts

Rent has been frequently referenced by various television shows, including *The Simpsons, Glee, The Big Bang Theory, Gilmore Girls, Seinfeld, Girls, Superstore,* and *Modern Family.* It has also inspired the genesis of other Broadway shows: The character Yitzhak in *Hedwig and the Angry Inch* speaks of his desire to play Angel, while Lin-Manuel Miranda has cited *Rent* as a source of inspiration while writing *In the Heights* and *Hamilton*!

NOMINATED TONYS
(ORIGINAL PRODUCTION)
10

WINNING TONYS
(ORIGINAL PRODUCTION)
4

GLASS

chilled coupe

---

2 oz. Western-
style gin

1½ oz. grapefruit
juice

1 oz. St-Germain
elderflower
liqueur

2 dashes
Peychaud's
bitters

GARNISH
expressed
grapefruit twist,
optional

La Vie Bohemian

SERVES 1   A rock musical loosely based on Giacomo Puccini's opera *La Bohème*, *Rent* premiered Off-Broadway on January 25, 1996, and the theatre world has been over the moon about it ever since. Following eight friends in Manhattan's East Village during the height of the city's HIV/AIDS crisis, the show arguably revolutionized Broadway, attracting devoted fans, known as "RENT-heads," who would camp out in front of the box office for deeply discounted night-of tickets. Critics were also fans, as the show received numerous accolades, including the 1996 Pulitzer Prize for Drama and the 1996 Tony Award for Best Musical.

While we can't be sure this cocktail will ward off the finance bros and gentrifiers who are raising your rent, we can promise you'll be feeling ready for anything after a few of our takes on the nouveau-classic bohemian cocktail. After a few, you might be inspired to go out tonight, or to travel all the way to sunny Santa Fe.

Combine all ingredients in a shaker tin over ice. Shake thoroughly to mix, chill, and dilute, then strain into chilled coupe. Express the grapefruit twist over the glass, then discard.

ENCORE

Add an egg white to the mixture, give a slightly harder shake, then after straining into the glass add a few extra dashes of Peychaud's bitters for aroma and color.

Little Shop of Horrors

MUSIC BY
Alan Menken

BOOK AND LYRICS BY
Howard Ashman

BROADWAY OPENING
October 2, 2003
AT THE
Virginia Theatre

WEST END OPENING
October 12, 1983
AT THE
Comedy Theatre

Fun Facts

The stage production of *Little Shop of Horrors* is based on the 1960 black comedy film of the same name. The show itself had a much more successful run Off-Broadway than on, playing from 1982 to 1987 at the Orpheum Theatre. A film version of the musical premiered in 1986, directed by Frank Oz and using one of his legendary puppets for Audrey II.

NOMINATED TONYS (ORIGINAL PRODUCTION)

1

GLASS

half-pint mason
jar (or class
it up a bit and
serve in a
champagne
flute)

---

1 oz. bourbon

½ oz. triple sec

6 dashes of
Angostura
or other
"aromatic"
bitters

6 dashes
Peychaud's
bitters

5 oz. grapefruit-
flavored hard
seltzer (see
note)

GARNISH
expressed
orange twist

Suddenly Seelbach!

SERVES 1 Flower-shop employee battles man-eating plant on the wrong side of the tracks. Yes, the tagline for the cult classic *Little Shop of Horrors* is rather far-fetched, but its toe-tapping score of rock, Motown, and doo-wop has secured its place in the hearts of musical lovers. With numerous Off-Broadway, West End, and touring company revivals, as well as two feature films, *Little Shop of Horrors* has proven to be a timeless staple on stage and screen.

And so what to make of the hero, Seymour Krelborn? Sure, he's a putz, but he's got drive, ambition, and a slightly twisted but kind heart. Luckily, there is a cocktail that mirrors his wily personality. While the "classic" Seelbach cocktail was in fact a bit of a poseur (often sold as having been around since the hotel's early days, it is in fact a modern invention, but that's a different story), it nonetheless is a delicious modern classic. Our delightfully Skid Row take can and should be enjoyed prior to dinner.

Combine all ingredients except the hard seltzer in a mixing glass over 4 ice cubes and stir to combine. Strain into your glassware, then float with the bubbly. Express the orange peel over the drink, drop it in, and embrace the aspirations of a Skid Row dreamer.

NOTE: This drink is generally much more approachable with sparkling wine so if you've got it handy, use it!

Little Shot of Horrors

chilled shot
glass

SERVES 1 Toe-tapping, tongue-in-cheek show tunes like
"Suddenly Seymour" and "Skid Row" might add flavor to the
show, but any Broadway buff will agree that the heart of *Little
Shop of Horrors* is Audrey II, a plant from outer space that
needs to consume human blood in order to survive. In almost
every major stage and screen adaptation, a puppeteering
team of at least two adults is required to operate Audrey II
effectively, while another actor supplies the voice. For the
1986 film, no less than puppet master general Frank Oz
himself designed "Twoey" and one of the principal operators
was Brian Henson, Jim Henson's eldest son. This fun and
crowd-pleasing party shot with quite a bite bears more than
a passing resemblance to a tiny Audrey II. Be forewarned:
This shot goes down easier than nitrous oxide and can quickly
leave you feeling no pain.

½ oz. vodka

¼ oz. Midori
liqueur

¼ oz. pineapple
juice (yes,
canned/bottled
is fine)

1 barspoon
heavy cream or
half and half,
optional

½ barspoon
grenadine

Carefully pour each ingredient in order as above into a
chilled shot glass. The cream (if you are using it) will seize
or "curdle," and the grenadine should enrobe it in a bright,
gory red-and-green layer. Shoot immediately, and slide on
down to Skid Row.

Once on This Island

MUSIC BY
Stephen Flaherty

BOOK AND LYRICS BY
Lynn Ahrens

BROADWAY OPENING
October 18, 1990
AT THE
Booth Theatre

WEST END OPENING
September 28, 1994
AT THE
West End Royalty Theatre

Fun Facts

The first Broadway revival premiered on December 3, 2017, at Circle in the Square Theatre. In addition to the theatre-in-the-round performance, the stage was covered in sand and throughout the show, several live animals, including goats and chickens, were used as "extras." The revival was nominated for eight Tonys, winning for Best Revival.

NOMINATED TONYS (ORIGINAL PRODUCTION)
8

Once on This Long Island Iced Tea

SERVES 1 In *Once on This Island*, four gods rule over an island in the Caribbean: Asaka, Agwé, Erzulie, and Papa Ge. The love story between Ti Moune and Daniel Beauxhomme unfolds because of a bet between Erzulie, the goddess of love, and Papa Ge, the demon of Death, to determine which of the two is stronger. In this Caribbean spin on the Long Island Iced Tea, four rums are combined with curaçao, lemon juice, and simple syrup to come together for a powerful cocktail indeed.

The musical production of *Once on This Island* was adapted from Rosa Guy's novel *My Love, My Love, or the Peasant Girl*, which in turn offered a Caribbean interpretation of Hans Christian Andersen's "The Little Mermaid," both using the narrative to explore themes of racism, classism, and colonialism. The island spirits may have fought in the musical, but you'll find they blend together smoothly here.

Although the Long Island has been the harbinger of many a hangover throughout its illustrious history, our trusted bartender hopes to redeem that reputation. Both in the interest of appealing to the refined palate of you, dear musical lover, and of honoring the French Caribbean settings of *Once on This Island*'s antagonist gods, we offer this blend of all island spirits in lieu of the vodka, gin, and tequila of the original. Oh, we definitely kept the rum, though.

This cocktail can be prepared directly in the serving glass by combining all ingredients except the cola, giving it a stir, then adding ice and cola to finish. Garnish and serve.

NOTE: Each of these rums (rhums) are distinctive and have been chosen to blend, so please try not to substitute.

ENCORE

For those who prefer the classic version, simply replace the Clément, Neisson, and Damoiseau with equal measures of vodka, gin, and blanco tequila. You may also substitute the dry curaçao with Cointreau or triple sec.

GLASS

collins

½ oz. Clément Rhum VSOP Rhum Agricole Vieux

½ oz. Neisson Rhum Agricole Blanc

½ oz. Damoiseau Virgin Cane rum

½ oz. Rhum J.M. Gold

½ oz. Pierre Ferrand Dry Curaçao

½ oz. lemon juice

½ oz. simple syrup

1 oz. of cola

GARNISH
lemon wedge

Oklahoma!

MUSIC BY
Richard Rodgers

BOOK AND LYRICS BY
Oscar Hammerstein II

BROADWAY OPENING
March 31, 1943
AT THE
St. James Theatre

WEST END OPENING
April 30, 1947
AT THE
Theatre Royal, Drury Lane

Fun Facts

The original Broadway production of *Oklahoma!* opened before the conception of the Tony Awards in 1947. That has not stopped it from garnering numerous accolades, however. Rodgers and Hammerstein won a Pulitzer Prize for the show in 1944, and numerous revivals both on Broadway and the West End have racked up nearly two dozen Tony and Olivier nominations.

GLASS

highball with
crushed ice

1½ oz. corn
whiskey

¾ oz. dry curaçao
or your favorite
orange liqueur

¾ oz. fresh lime
juice

½ oz. orgeat
syrup

½ oz. dark rum

GARNISH
lime wheel
and a nice
mint bouquet.
If you have a
paper umbrella
handy, by all
means use it.

Oh, What a Beautiful Mai Tai

SERVES 1   A classic from the equally classic duo Rodgers and Hammerstein, *Oklahoma!* first had a beautiful morning on Broadway in 1943, opening at the St. James Theatre to critical acclaim and running for five years. A story of love, jealousy, and hardship set in the 1906 Oklahoma Indian Territory, the show's operatic score and elaborate dance interludes— including a fifteen-minute sequence titled the "Dream Ballet"—charmed critics and lay audiences alike. The show has been revived and revamped countless times across the globe, including a much-lauded, groundbreaking 2019 Broadway revival that emphasized the show's darker undertones. (Perhaps the most notable achievement of this revival was Ali Stroker's win for Best Featured Actress, making her the first wheelchair user to ever win a Tony Award.)

The king of tiki cocktails likely originated in a tiny Bay Area bar right around the same time that *Oklahoma!* took to the Broadway stage. (Ironically, the rise of "exotica" would bring *South Pacific* to the stage less than a decade later.) Our version swaps out the rum for a more familiar spirit to folks from the Sooner State, though it's no less tropical or delicious. In tiki terms, this iteration is technically a Honi Honi, but don't let that put a hitch in your surrey. Our bartender guarantees that it's a cocktail that you cain't say no to enjoying.

Combine all ingredients except the rum in a shaker tin over ice. Shake hard until the tin lightly frosts over, then strain into the crushed-ice-filled glass. Finally, pour the dark rum just over the drink's surface to create a layered effect. Perch the lime wheel on the glass, give the mint a smack to wake it up, then nestle it alongside.

Sunset Blvd.

MUSIC BY
Andrew
Lloyd Webber

BOOK AND LYRICS BY
Don Black and
Christopher Hampton

BROADWAY OPENING
November 17,
1994
AT THE
Minskoff
Theatre

WEST END OPENING
July 12,
1993
AT THE
Adelphi
Theatre

Fun Facts

Based on the 1950 Billy Wilder film of the same name, the musical adaptation of *Sunset Blvd.* was pursued and abandoned by Stephen Sondheim in the 1960s and a possible film remake starring Angela Lansbury was also considered.

NOMINATED TONYS
(ORIGINAL PRODUCTION)
11

WINNING TONYS
(ORIGINAL PRODUCTION)
7

GLASS

highball

2 oz. white
tequila

2½ oz. grapefruit
juice

½ oz. grenadine
or pomegranate
molasses

2 oz. soda water

GARNISH
quartered slice
of grapefruit or
orange slice

Tequila Sunset Blvd.

SERVES 1 While the talkies may have left Norma Desmond behind, musical theatre certainly hasn't. The 1950 classic film *Sunset Boulevard* has inspired adaptations across the globe, premiering on the West End in 1993 and making its way across the pond to Broadway in 1994. Iconic divas Patti LuPone and Glenn Close have each taken their turns as the ill-fated silver screen star, and both received critical acclaim for their efforts. With a score by Broadway legend Andrew Lloyd Webber, the show is a worthy vechicle for any actress stepping into the shoes of the "Greatest Movie Star of All."

This mix between a Paloma and a classic tequila sunrise would've certainly kept Norma in good spirits. Beautifully simple and great any time of day or night.

Combine the tequila and grapefruit juice directly in the glass, give a quick stir, then add ice. In a separate vessel, gently mix the grenadine and soda water together, then slowly pour directly onto the top of the ice cubes to create a layered effect with the pink/red "sunset" now on top. Garnish with the grapefruit slice or orange.

NOTE: White grapefruit will give the best visual effect, but ruby red will still make a delicious cocktail. If you can't have grapefruit juice for dietary reasons, good fresh orange juice will be a lovely substitute.

Sunset Boulevardier

SERVES 1 Ready for a close-up? Norma Desmond is too grand a star to only inspire one drink in our collection. So, enter the Sunset Boulevardier, a brawnier whiskey-based cousin of the Negroni, perfect from the first chilly gusts of September all the way through to the last rains of April. For a Hollywood twist befitting one of the biggest wine-producing regions in the world, add a robust sweet vermouth from the San Joaquin Valley.

Combine all ingredients in a mixing glass over ice. Stir thoroughly to combine, then strain into the Nick 'n' Nora coupe (or single rocks glass over a few ice cubes), and express the orange twist over the drink and drop it in.

ENCORE
To execute this cocktail as an all-American affair, substitute St. George Distilling Bruto for the Campari.

GLASS

Nick 'n' Nora or small coupe, chilled. If you prefer your boulevardier on the rocks, a single rocks glass.

1½ oz. rye whiskey

¾ oz. Campari

¾ oz. sweet vermouth

GARNISH expressed orange twist

An American in Paris

MUSIC BY
George Gershwin

BOOK BY
Craig Lucas

LYRICS BY
Ira Gershwin

BROADWAY OPENING
April 12, 2015
AT THE
Palace Theatre

WEST END OPENING
March 21, 2017
AT THE
Dominion Theatre

Fun Facts

True to the plot of the musical, the stage adaptation of *An American in Paris* had its world premiere at the Théâtre du Châtelet in Paris on December 10, 2014. The principal members of the cast reprised their roles for the Broadway premiere.

NOMINATED TONYS
(ORIGINAL PRODUCTION)
12

WINNING TONYS
(ORIGINAL PRODUCTION)
4

An Americano in Paris

highball

---

1 oz. St.
George Bruto
Americano

1 oz. Dolin Rouge
vermouth

A splash of dry
sparkling wine

GARNISH
orange slice

SERVES 1 Although best remembered as the classic 1951 Gene Kelly and Leslie Caron flick, *An American in Paris* was adapted for the stage in late 2014 and premiered on the Great White Way in April 2015. Recounting the thwarted love affair between American war vet Jerry Mulligan and the cultured Parisian Lise, the film *An American in Paris* was lauded for its lush ballet interludes, and the stage version did not disappoint even the most enthusiastic of balletgoers. With an original cast helmed by New York Ballet principal Robert Fairchild and Royal Ballet first artist Leanne Cope, the show was acclaimed as "S' Wonderful" by critics, and pirouetted its way to several Tony nominations, including a win for choreographer and director Christopher Wheeldon.

While the Americano is one of the best-known and popular aperitifs in Italian history, having been served by no less a titan than Gaspare Campari himself, our version makes use of an American bitter liquor, a French sweet vermouth, and champagne's lesser-known cousin crémant to round out the cast and add a little extra pop. You'll certainly feel like you've got rhythm after drinking a few of these.

Fill highball glass with ice, combine the St. George, Dolin Rouge, and finally the splash of bubbly, drop in the orange slice, give it a light stir, and enjoy, ideally in dappled sunshine in the late afternoon, though your bartender is fond of an Americano as a brunch cocktail as well.

NOTE: Cocktail purists would argue that the addition of sparkling wine technically makes this a *sbagliato*, and they would be correct! At any rate, for the purists, substitute soda water instead of sparkling wine.

The Wiz

BOOK BY
William F. Brown

LYRICS BY
Charlie Smalls, Zachary Walzer, and Luther Vandross

MUSIC BY
Charlie Smalls, Timothy Graphenreed, Harold Wheeler, George Faison, and Luther Vandross

BROADWAY OPENING
January 5, 1975
AT THE
Majestic Theatre

WEST END OPENING
December 11, 1984
AT THE
Lyric Hammersmith Theatre

NOMINATED TONYS (ORIGINAL PRODUCTION)
8

WINNING TONYS (ORIGINAL PRODUCTION)
7

GLASS

chilled collins
or highball

---

2 oz. Wenneker
Elderflower
dry gin (If
you can't find
Wenneker,
substitute
1¾ oz. dry
gin and ¼ oz.
elderflower
liqueur.)

¾ oz. fresh
lemon juice

¾ oz. strawberry
simple syrup
(see recipe
next page)

1 egg white

Cold soda water
to finish

GARNISH
sliced
strawberry,
optional

The Gin Whiz

SERVES 1 *The Wiz* is a great classic to return to time and again, whether you've never been south of 125th Street or you've eased on down the road to Oz and back. Broadway star Stephanie Mills took that lesson to heart, starring as Dorothy Gale in the original 1974 production, and then returning as Aunt Em more than forty years later for the 2015 television special *The Wiz Live!* The Gin Whiz won't keep quite that long, although the strawberry simple syrup recipe should see you through for up to a month.

This slippery smooth take on the classic Gin Fizz pays homage to *The Wiz*'s urban fantasy spin on *The Wizard of Oz*, featuring an all-Black cast. Elderflower and strawberry provide the Gin Whiz a burst of contrast, color, and aroma to the classic drink. This intoxicating floral perfume offers a nod to the source material's iconic poppies without including them in the mix: There may be no place like home, but the Gin Whiz shouldn't send you into eternal slumber.

Combine all ingredients in a shaker tin, add 5 to 6 ice cubes, seal tightly, and shake hard for up to a minute. Not only are you chilling the drink by doing this, you are also creating an egg-white foam that gives any fizz worth its name such a distinctive look. Carefully strain the cocktail into a chilled collins or highball glass. It'll be about half full. Then carefully pour soda water along one side of the glass to fizz the drink without disrupting that hard-won foam!

Strawberry Simple Syrup

MAKES ENOUGH FOR APPROXIMATELY 10 TO 12 DRINKS

Combine in a small saucepan and bring it to a boil while
stirring, then lower to a simmer for 10 to 15 minutes or
until the strawberries begin to get soft. (Underripe fruit
will still work for this recipe—it'll just take longer.) Remove
from heat and cool for about ten minutes. Strain through
a fine-mesh sieve or a double layer of cheesecloth in a
colander. Store the syrup in an airtight container in the
fridge. Batch will keep for about a month.

1½ cups hulled
    and sliced
    strawberries

1 cup white sugar

1 cup water

Annie Get Your Gun

MUSIC AND LYRICS BY
Irving Berlin

BOOK BY
Dorothy Fields and
Herbert Fields

BROADWAY OPENING
May 16, 1946
AT THE
Imperial
Theatre

WEST END OPENING
June 7, 1947
AT THE
London
Coliseum

Fun Facts

Despite premiering too early to take home any Tony
Awards for its original run, *Annie Get Your Gun*'s 1999
Broadway revival won Best Revival of a Musical and Best
Actress for Bernadette Peters. The revival cast also won a
Grammy Award for Best Musical Show Album.

Annie, Get Your Gin

SERVES 1 There's really no business like show business, as any true theatre lover knows all too well. Inspired by the life of legendary sharpshooter Annie Oakley, *Annie Get Your Gun* opened at Broadway's Imperial Theatre in 1946, running for more than 1,400 performances and inspiring countless revivals and a beloved Hollywood release. Music and lyrics by Irving Berlin helped to craft one of the most iconic scores of all time, and stage legends including Ethel Merman, Mary Martin, and Bernadette Peters have each taken their turn toting Annie's rifle.

Our salute to Annie is an Americanized version of the Suffering Bastard cocktail concocted in World War II–era Egypt and inspired by her husband and fellow sharpshooter, Frank Butler. It features whiskey, as that spirit would've been much easier to lay hands on than brandy while on tour with Buffalo Bill's Wild West Show. An excellent restorative as most mule (booze, lime, ginger) variants tend to be, but also a nice predinner cocktail.

Combine gin, bourbon, lime juice, and bitters in your shaker tin over ice. Shake to combine and strain into your collins glass. Add ice and ginger beer, then garnish with the lime wheel.

GLASS

chilled collins

---

1 oz. Western-style gin

1 oz. bourbon (Buffalo Trace is the preferred brand, of course—Bill wouldn't have it any other way.)

½ oz. lime juice

2 dashes Angostura bitters

Ginger beer to float (or ginger ale in a pinch)

GARNISH
lime wheel

GLASS

Nick 'n' Nora
or small coupe,
chilled

1 oz. Angostura
bitters

½ oz. overproof
rum

1 oz. Velvet
Falernum

¾ oz. lime juice

GARNISH
dehydrated
lime wheel or
very thin sliced
fresh lime
wheel, optional

Anything You Can Do, I Can Do Bitters

SERVES 1 *Annie Get Your Gun* is certainly not at a loss for iconic numbers. With showstoppers like "There's No Business Like Show Business," "You Can't Get a Man with a Gun," and "They Say It's Wonderful," the soundtrack is a staple in the repertoire of any theatre geek. Its eleven o'clock number, "Anything You Can Do," which highlights the professional rivalry between Annie and Frank, is arguably the most memorable tune in the musical, and has been reproduced, repurposed, and reimagined by stars spanning the decades, from Judy Garland and Bing Crosby, to Miss Piggy and Neil Patrick Harris.

This cocktail is our own delightful twist on a modern classic, with a tip of the hat to Giuseppe González. A rum-infused version of a Trinidad Sour, it takes advantage of the depth and complexity of Angostura while still delivering a highly sippable and sophisticated cocktail. It's the perfect cocktail to imbibe while engaged in a competitive tete-a-tete with your own sharpshooting rival.

Combine all ingredients into a shaker tin over 4 to 5 good ice cubes and shake hard until tin is lightly frosted. Strain into chilled glass and, if using, rest a carefully placed dehydrated lime wheel garnish on the surface.

NOTE: Velvet Falernum can be substituted with orgeat syrup, though the resulting beverage will be a little softer and nuttier. Many even prefer this version.

Wicked

MUSIC AND LYRICS BY
Stephen Schwartz

BOOK BY
Winnie Holzman

BROADWAY OPENING
October 30, 2003
AT THE
Gershwin Theatre

WEST END OPENING
September 26, 2006
AT THE
Apollo Victoria Theatre

Fun Facts

In a nod to its source material, the musical contains a subtle homage to *The Wizard of Oz*. The first few bars of the "Unlimited" theme closely resemble the opening of "Over the Rainbow."

NOMINATED TONYS
(ORIGINAL PRODUCTION)
10

WINNING TONYS
(ORIGINAL PRODUCTION)
3

Defying Grenadine

SERVES 1   Need a show and libation that the whole family can enjoy? Then perennial family favorite *Wicked* might be just what you need to make you and yours feel like you're dancing through life. A retelling of the children's classic *The Wizard of Oz* from the perspective of Elphaba, the Wicked Witch of the West, the show premiered on Broadway in 2003, and as of this writing is Broadway's fifth-longest-running show and second-highest grossing (behind another longtime family favorite, *The Lion King*). Its cast alums comprise enough Broadway legends to have their own wall at Sardi's, and the original company alone includes stars such as Idina Menzel, Kristin Chenoweth, Joel Grey, Norbert Leo Butz, and Carole Shelley. With a rousing, thematic, and downright catchy score and themes like true love and even truer friendship, it's a show sure to stir emotion in anyone, even if they're not a sentimental man.

Our Oz-inspired version of the soda fountain classic Roy Rogers is much less sweet but still "popular" with the junior set. Store-bought grenadine will work, though for a much brighter and more nuanced flavor, follow the recipe on the next page for making your own grenadine syrup. Kept in a sealed jar and chilled, it keeps as long as a run of *Wicked* on Broadway.

Build directly in the glass over ice by pouring cola until the glass is almost full, then adding the grenadine. Give it a quick stir to combine, drop in the cherry, then serve with a flourish and maybe a fancy striped straw.

ENCORE
Want a Ginger Rogers? Swap the cola for ginger ale. Want a Shirley Temple? Let lemon-lime soda step in instead. Good grenadine will elevate many a simple beverage.

NOTE: Some cocktail cherries contain alcohol, so if that's a concern, use a sundae cherry instead or even a lemon twist.

GLASS

collins glass

---

8 oz. dry cola

½–1 oz. grenadine, depending on how sweet you want your mocktail

---

GARNISH
cherry

Grenadine

MAKES ABOUT 3 CUPS OR ENOUGH FOR ABOUT 40 COCKTAILS

2 cups
pomegranate
juice

2 cups sugar

3–4 dashes (about
½ teaspoon)
orange flower
water

In a large saucepan over medium heat combine the
pomegranate juice and sugar, and stir until fully dissolved.
Allow mixture to come to a slow boil, then reduce the heat,
cover, and simmer for 10–15 minutes. Remove from heat
and allow to cool uncovered. The mixture will thicken
slightly. Once it's cooled, pour the syrup into a clean glass
bottle and add the orange flower water sparingly as it's a
very potent ingredient. Seal the bottle, give it a shake, and
you're all set! Kept refrigerated, grenadine will keep pretty
much indefinitely.

Hairspray

MUSIC AND LYRICS BY
Marc Shaiman and Scott Wittman

BOOK BY
Mark O'Donnell and Thomas Meehan

BROADWAY OPENING
August 15, 2002
AT THE
Neil Simon Theatre

WEST END OPENING
October 30, 2007
AT THE
Shaftesbury Theatre

Fun Facts

The fictional *Corny Collins Show* featured in the musical is a riff on the real-life *Buddy Deane Show*, which was inspired by the popular dance show *American Bandstand*.

NOMINATED TONYS
(ORIGINAL PRODUCTION)
13

WINNING TONYS
(ORIGINAL PRODUCTION)
8

Good Morning Boilermaker

SERVES 1 Hey, theatre lover, welcome to the sixties with the bopping 2002 musical *Hairspray*. Plus-size teen with a dream Tracy Turnblad shows that barriers are made to be broken when she earns a place on 1960s Baltimore-based dance show *The Corny Collins Show* and eventually helps integrate it as well. Based on the 1988 film of the same name, the original Broadway run of *Hairspray* won eight Tony awards, including Best Musical, and also earned critical acclaim across the pond, earning the Olivier Award for Best Musical. With toe-tapping tunes like "Run and Tell That" and "You Can't Stop the Beat," *Hairspray* is an upbeat, feel-good show that the entire family can get behind.

To honor that energetic feeling that *Hairspray* gives, we've got an eye-opening, coffee-forward take on the classic boilermaker for those of you who maybe don't roll out of bed with Tracy Turnblad energy. While our version lacks the knockdown of the classic high-proof bourbon-and-a-beer combo, this sweet sipper is a great way to perk up or mellow out, suitable for brunch or as an after-show dessert drink.

While there's no wrong way to drink a boilermaker (and we want you to embrace your own style), our bartender would caution against dropping the shot glass into the beer. The inevitable smack in the teeth from the shot glass falling into your face while drinking from the pint isn't a good look. Rather, pour the shot into the beer and enjoy at a more leisurely pace.

GLASS

chilled pint and shot glass

---

1 bottle (or can) of a coffee porter, stout, or brown ale

1½ oz. Frangelico, Kahlúa, or Baileys

GARNISH a few coffee beans resting on the head of the beer

Mamma Mia!

MUSIC AND LYRICS BY
Benny Andersson and
Björn Ulvaeus

BOOK BY
Catherine
Johnson

BROADWAY OPENING
October 18,
2001
AT THE
Winter
Garden
Theatre

WEST END OPENING
April 6,
1999
AT THE
Prince
Edward
Theatre

Fun Facts

Aside from being a hit both on Broadway and the West End, *Mamma Mia!* has dazzled audiences across the world, opening in locales as diverse as China, Poland, South Africa, Spain, and Argentina, along with more than forty other countries on six continents.

**NOMINATED TONYS
(ORIGINAL
PRODUCTION)**
5

Honey, Honey, Money, Money, Money

SERVES 1 Although it wasn't Swedish pop quartet ABBA's first foray into musical theatre—Benny Andersson and Björn Ulvaeus composed the music for *Chess*—*Mamma Mia!* was their most popular entry by far. The jukebox musical is the seventh-longest-running production in West End history and the ninth longest in Broadway history. Incorporating some of the group's most popular songs, including "Gimme! Gimme! (A Man after Midnight)," "Take a Chance on Me," and "Waterloo," the show discoed its way into the hearts of Broadway buffs everywhere.

So get your dancing queen on while drinking this sweet classic inspired by London's and New York's exclusive Milk and Honey bar.

Combine all ingredients in a shaker tin over ice, shake hard until the tin is frosted over, then strain into your chilled glass. Express the lemon twist over the glass, then rest on the rim. Much like a daiquiri, it should be drunk swiftly.

GLASS

Nick 'n' Nora or small coupe, chilled

2 oz. rye whiskey

1 oz. honey simple syrup

¾ oz. lemon juice

GARNISH
expressed
lemon twist

Annie

MUSIC BY
Charles
Strouse

BOOK BY
Thomas
Meehan

LYRICS BY
Martin
Charnin

BROADWAY OPENING
April 21, 1977
AT THE
Alvin
Theatre

WEST END OPENING
May 3, 1978
AT THE
Victoria Palace
Theatre

Fun Facts

The musical was novelized by Thomas Meehan and published in 1980, with a reprint issued in 2014. The novel adapted numerous lyrics into dialogue and expanded the backgrounds of the main characters, exploring the physical and emotional abuse that Miss Hannigan inflicted on her charges.

NOMINATED TONYS
(ORIGINAL PRODUCTION)
10

WINNING TONYS
(ORIGINAL PRODUCTION)
7

GLASS

double old-
fashioned or
highball

1½ oz. vodka

3 oz. fresh
clementine
juice

¼ oz. lemon juice

½ oz. Spice
Bomb liqueur
(Galliano or
sambuca,
plus a drop of
vanilla extract,
will work as
well.)

GARNISH
orange twist,
optional

The Daddy Warbanger

SERVES 1 The tale of a plucky little orphan with a heart of gold, *Annie* first graced the Great White Way in 1977. It successfully ran for six years, spawned numerous subsequent revivals and national tours, and inspired a feature film adaption in 1982, which at the time was the most expensive musical ever made. (Talk about a hard-knock life for the producer's pocketbooks.) Over the years, and no doubt due to its score—which features crowd-pleasers like "N.Y.C." and tearjerkers like "Tomorrow"—the show has maintained an iconic status in popular culture, referenced in numerous films and television shows, including *Friends*, *The X-Files*, *Full House*, and *30 Rock*.

With a drink opulent yet manly enough for Annie's adoptive parent, Daddy Warbucks, our gourmet take on the Harvey Wallbanger makes good use of the year-round availability of clementine oranges and a nicely spiced liqueur to raise this former nightclub staple to the lofty standards of a tycoon. After one or two of these, you'll be cruising down easy street for sure.

Combine the vodka, the clementine juice, and the lemon juice in a mixing tin over ice. Shake thoroughly to chill and dilute, then strain into your glass over fresh ice. Finally, pour the spice bomb over the back of a spoon placed just above the drink's surface to create a layered effect. If using, express the orange twist over the glass, then drop in the drink.

The Music Man

MUSIC AND LYRICS BY
Meredith
Willson

BOOK BY
Meredith Willson and
Franklin Lacey

BROADWAY OPENING
December 19,
1957
AT THE
Majestic
Theatre

WEST END OPENING
March 16,
1961
AT THE
Adelphi
Theatre

Fun Facts

The Music Man has been spoofed or referenced
in multiple television shows, including *Family Guy*,
The Simpsons, and *Grace & Frankie*.

NOMINATED TONYS
(ORIGINAL PRODUCTION)

9

WINNING TONYS
(ORIGINAL PRODUCTION)

5

GLASS

collins

---

2 oz. sarsaparilla syrup (see recipe next page)

¼ tsp. fresh grated ginger (optional)

6–8 oz. club soda or seltzer

GARNISH
orange wheel

Shipoopi Sasper

SERVES 1 Seventy-six trombones and 110 cornets led the way for con man Harold Hill when he arrived in fictional River City, Iowa, and on the real-life Broadway stage in 1957's *The Music Man*. Just as Harold won the heart of River City's librarian, Marian, audiences and critics alike were won over by the show's catchy tunes and small-town Americana charm. The show garnered numerous accolades, including the 1957 Tony Award for Best Musical (notably beating out *West Side Story*, which opened five months prior), as well as the first-ever Grammy Award for Musical Theatre Album.

This soda-fountain throwback right out of River City can be enjoyed with or without alcohol. Now while you could skip the syrup recipe below for store-bought, well, then you got Trouble with a capital T, which rhymes with P and that stands for Premade. While the ingredient list may seem daunting, the actual method is straightforward and can be a great project to keep the little ones busy on a Saturday. You don't want them wandering down to a pool hall, after all.

Build directly in the glass by combining the syrup, grated ginger, and about half the soda, and stir to combine. Then add ice and additional soda to float. Pop in the orange wheel (paper straw optional) and have a swell sipper. If the texture of the grated ginger puts you off, prior to adding the ice run the mixture through a fine-mesh strainer, then proceed.

ENCORE

For an adult variation, this is lovely with 1½ oz. of either bourbon or rum added in. Of course, the townsfolk might not approve.

Sarsaparilla Syrup

MAKES ENOUGH FOR 10 TO 12 DRINKS

In a medium saucepan combine all ingredients except
the sarsaparilla extract and bring to a low boil over
medium-high heat. Reduce the heat to a simmer, cover,
then set a timer for 35 minutes. Next remove the lid,
add the extract, then simmer uncovered for an additional
5 minutes. Remove from the heat and let cool completely
before transferring to a clean, resealable container.
Kept refrigerated, your sarsaparilla syrup will keep
for up to a month.

½ vanilla bean
(about 3 inches
long)

5 whole allspice
berries

3 whole cloves

1 cinnamon stick
(about 3 inches
long)

¼ tsp. whole
fennel seeds

¼ tsp. whole white
peppercorns

3 tbsp. raisins

3 dates, pitted

3 tbsp. maple
syrup

1 tsp. molasses

4 cups water

1 tbsp.
sarsaparilla
extract

Hamilton

MUSIC, BOOK, AND LYRICS BY

Lin-Manuel Miranda

BROADWAY OPENING

August 6, 2015

AT THE

Richard Rodgers Theatre

WEST END OPENING

December 21, 2017

AT THE

Victoria Palace Theatre

Fun Facts

With sixteen total Tony nominations, *Hamilton* is the most-nominated show in history. Its eleven wins make it the second-most decorated show, suprassed only by *The Producers*, which had twelve wins.

NOMINATED TONYS
(ORIGINAL PRODUCTION)

16

WINNING TONYS
(ORIGINAL PRODUCTION)

11

HAMILTON

GLASS

chilled coupe or
cocktail glass

---

1 oz. brandy

1 oz. crème de
cacao (either
light or dark)

1 oz. half-and-
half (see note)

GARNISH
freshly grated
nutmeg

Brandy Alexander Hamilton

SERVES 1 In 1791, Secretary of the Treasury Alexander Hamilton proposed a tax on distilled spirits to help combat the rising national debt. Three years later, President George Washington found himself leading a militia of more than 12,000 federal soldiers to quash an armed rebellion in western Pennsylvania. This was the first and only time a sitting US president personally led soldiers in an active campaign, in what came to be known as the Whiskey Rebellion.

While Lin-Manuel Miranda's musical *Hamilton* skimmed past this historic event in the Broadway rendition of "One Last Time," its Off-Broadway predecessor dedicated a song to the president's fighting spirits with "One Last Ride." Luckily, Alexander Hamilton's staunch opposition to affordable cocktails was cut from the musical, so you can enjoy this chocolaty dessert cocktail guilt free. So, raise a glass to freedom from songs about taxation, and raise a couple more to the American Revolution.

You can even pour an extra shot of brandy as a treat while you're mixing up this classic drink. Whether you throw it away or throw it back is up to you—after all, no one else was in the room where it happened, so nobody *needs* to know.

While the Brandy Alexander didn't come to prominence until the early years of the twentieth century, its friendly flavors, suitable for after dinner or holiday drinks, would've been welcome at a Revolution-era table or fifth-floor walk-up in the West Village. Our version maintains the equal portions ratio of the original, though we dispense with the heavy cream for a slightly lighter option.

Combine all ingredients over ice in a shaker, shaking hard to incorporate until the tin frosts over slightly. (Dairy needs a little more elbow grease to mix properly.) Strain into your chilled glass and carefully grate the nutmeg over the top.

ENCORE

For an even more old-school variation, or if brandy isn't available, the original "Alexander" cocktail utilized gin instead. Give it a go: They are all lovely for different reasons.

NOTE: For a vegan or dairy-free option, an extra-creamy oat milk is a great choice. You'll want to add it to the shaker of ice first, then add the crème de cacao, and finally the brandy. This will help minimize the oat milk separating. No worries: If it does, it'll still taste great, but the texture and appearance will be affected.

Gypsy

MUSIC BY
Jule Styne

BOOK BY
Arthur Laurents

LYRICS BY
Stephen Sondheim

BROADWAY OPENING
May 21, 1959
AT THE
Broadway Theatre

WEST END OPENING
May 29, 1973
AT THE
Piccadilly Theatre

Fun Facts

The complicated character of Rose has been interpreted in a variety of ways by those involved in various productions of the musical. Takes range from monster-like (Walter Kerr) to misunderstood and traumatized (Bernadette Peters).

NOMINATED TONYS (ORIGINAL PRODUCTION)

8

Everything's Coming Up Rosé

SERVES 1 Inspired by the memoirs of strip tease artist Gypsy Rose Lee, the musical *Gypsy* centers on her mother, Rose, the ultimate stage mom. A passion project of theatre grand dame Ethel Merman, the show premiered on Broadway on May 21, 1959, with Merman originating the role of Rose. The role has been a staple of leading ladies since, with the likes of Angela Lansbury, Bernadette Peters, Patti LuPone, and Imelda Staunton all taking turns proclaiming that it's Rose's turn.

Ethel Merman would be pleased as . . . well, not punch (that's a different recipe), but happy to have this tasty tipple attached to her signature tune with its showstopping good looks. While I can't guarantee the world will be served up on a plate, after a couple of these you'll be swell, possibly great!

Combine all ingredients except soda in a shaker tin over ice and give a quick shake to combine and chill. Strain onto fresh ice in your collins glass, then top with soda, give a gentle stir, and garnish.

NOTES: Lillet rosé is the go-to here, though if you can't lay hands on it, Lustau Vermut is an able understudy.

If you couldn't find Lillet, you may need to add a bit more simple syrup to balance the cocktail.

Orange flower water is a wonderful substitute for rosewater.

GLASS

collins

1½ oz. rosé vermouth

¾ oz. London dry gin

¾ oz. lemon juice

½ oz. simple syrup

1 dash rosewater

Soda water to fill

GARNISH
an edible-grade rose petal would be tip-top, but a lemon twist would be grand too

Chicago

MUSIC BY
John
Kander

BOOK BY
Fred Ebb and
Bob Fosse

LYRICS BY
Fred
Ebb

BROADWAY OPENING
June 3, 1975
AT THE
46th Street
Theatre

WEST END OPENING
April 10, 1979
AT THE
Cambridge
Theatre

Fun Facts

Although it is clearly sensational, the musical is in fact based on real-life events. The characters of Roxie Hart and Velma Kelly were inspired by accused murderesses Beulah Annan and Belva Gaertner, respectively, who were both covered as celebrities by Chicago press and were eventually acquitted.

NOMINATED TONYS (ORIGINAL PRODUCTION)
11

They Both Reached for the Gin

SERVES 1 *Chicago*, a jazz musical about two merry murderesses who get away with it, is a Broadway staple like no other. The Great White Way's longest-running revival, it's a show that even theatrical novices can at least hum a tune or two from. (The West End revival is equally iconic, as it holds the notable distinction of being the longest-running American show in the UK.) From the classic opener "All That Jazz" to the equally lush finale "Nowadays/Hot Honey Rag," Broadway theatregoers for generations have been razzle dazzled by the antics of Velma Kelly and Roxie Hart, as they perform the legendary Bob Fosse's seminal choreography.

A musical as famed as *Chicago* deserves a drink that matches its potency, and our bartender has one that will not disappoint. This rousing rendition of the 1920s favorite fizz splits our base spirit between London dry gin and sloe gin. (Technically not a gin at all but a gin-based liqueur flavored with sloe berries and sweetened.) Billy Flynn himself likely would've been no stranger to this potent tipple.

Combine all ingredients except seltzer in shaker tin, add ice, seal tight, and shake hard until tin has lightly frosted over, then strain into the collins glass over fresh ice. Finally, pour the seltzer carefully down the side of the glass to mix and fill. Top with the lemon wheel.

ENCORE
For a showier presentation and more robust texture, after combining other ingredients, add an egg white to the shaker, shake to chill and emulsify the drink, then strain off the ice and continue shaking the mixture to create a foam, then carry on as before.

GLASS

collins

---

1 oz. Plymouth sloe gin

1 oz. London dry gin

½ oz. simple syrup

¾ oz. fresh lemon juice

Seltzer to fill

GARNISH
lemon wheel

All That Jack 'n' Coke

SERVES 1 For taking in Broadway's longest-running revival, you're going to need a drink to take you into Act II, don't you think? After all, you can't do it alone. So, our trusty bartender has concocted a twist on a classic drink that is good to Mama Morton and will be good to you too. While nowadays the "jack 'n' coke" is exactly as described—highball, ice, whiskey, coke, and maybe a lemon wedge—for an elevated cocktail more at home in the glamorous hand of Velma Kelly than in a dive bar or college dorm room, try this variation.

Combine the bourbon, cola syrup, and bitters in a mixing glass over ice. Stir thoroughly to combine, chill, and slightly dilute, then strain into the Nick 'n' Nora or coupe. If using, express the lemon twist over the glass, then discard.

GLASS

Nick 'n' Nora or small coupe, chilled

2 oz. bourbon (a softer, wheated whiskey is great for this cocktail)

½ oz. cola syrup

1–2 dashes tiki bitters (Angostura will work great as well)

GARNISH
expressed lemon twist, optional

The Sound of Music

MUSIC BY
Richard Rodgers

LYRICS BY
Oscar Hammerstein II

BOOK BY
Howard Lindsay and Russel Crouse

BROADWAY OPENING
November 16, 1959
AT THE
Lunt Fontanne Theatre

WEST END OPENING
May 18, 1961
AT THE
Palace Theatre

NOMINATED TONYS
(ORIGINAL PRODUCTION)
9

WINNING TONYS
(ORIGINAL PRODUCTION)
5

Sixteen Going on Seventeen (Proof)

SERVES 1 The hills are truly alive in the Rodgers and Hammerstein musical *The Sound of Music*, the final collaboration that this duo created before Hammerstein's passing. Although it is best known for the beloved 1965 Julie Andrews and Christopher Plummer cinematic adaptation, the von Trapp family got their start on Broadway in 1959 at the Lunt-Fontanne Theatre, with Mary Martin and Theodore Bikel as Maria and Captain von Trapp. Although it was panned by critics upon its premiere, audiences felt otherwise; *The Sound of Music* has remained one of the "favorite things" of Broadway buffs across the globe and through the years, as generations have been inspired to climb every mountain and solve a problem like Maria.

This bracing, Alpine riff off the Americano is a good reminder that, although it's third on the playbill, the Génépi will have you running through mountain meadows without losing yourself due to the cocktail's lower overall alcohol content without sacrificing flavor.

Fill a highball glass with ice, then pour soda water about a quarter of the way up the glass. Add remaining ingredients, then soda on top to float. Give a gentle stir to incorporate, then garnish with an expressed lemon twist.

GLASS

highball

Club soda to fill

1½ oz. sweet vermouth

¾ oz. dry vermouth

¾ oz. Dolin Génépi des Alpes vermouth

GARNISH
expressed lemon twist

Evita

MUSIC BY
Andrew Lloyd Webber

BOOK AND LYRICS BY
Tim Rice

BROADWAY OPENING
September 25, 1979
AT THE
Broadway Theatre

WEST END OPENING
June 21, 1978
AT THE
Prince Edward Theatre

Fun Facts

The duo of Lloyd Webber and Rice originally developed *Evita* as a concept album, as they had done for *Jesus Christ Superstar*.

NOMINATED TONYS
(ORIGINAL PRODUCTION)
11

WINNING TONYS
(ORIGINAL PRODUCTION)
7

GLASS

Nick 'n' Nora
or small coupe,
chilled

1½ oz. vodka

1 oz. apple eau
de vie or apple
schnapps

½ oz. apple
brandy

GARNISH
thin slice of
green apple or
a dehydrated
slice of apple

Don't Cry for Me, Appletini

SERVES 1   It was truly a new Argentina from 1946 to 1952 under President Juan Perón and his iconic first lady, Eva, lovingly called Evita by the masses. Her larger, legendary rise to power was brought to life with Tim Rice and Andrew Lloyd Webber's equally beloved rock opera *Evita*. First opening on the West End in 1978, it transferred to Broadway a year later, with a young Patti LuPone in the title role, Mandy Patinkin as narrator figure Che, and Bob Gunton as President Juan Perón.

Our nod to *Evita* salutes the show's signature number, and is a tweaked classic based on the Hanky Panky from London's Savoy Hotel's heyday. It's sweet but not cloying, as well as herbaceous and slightly minty.

Combine all ingredients in a shaker tin, add ice, and shake hard to combine, chill, and dilute. Strain into your chilled glass, then pop on the apple garnish. (Our trusty bartender likes to set it against the rim, like a jaunty cap.) Careful, though—they pack a kick. Serve a few to guests for your Tony Awards viewing party, and you'll be saying oh, what a circus in no time.

Cinderella

BOOK BY
Oscar Hammerstein II
and Douglas Carter Beane

MUSIC BY
Richard
Rodgers

LYRICS BY
Oscar
Hammerstein II

BROADWAY OPENING
March 13,
2013
AT THE
Broadway
Theatre

Fun Facts
Although the musical *Cinderella*
had not appeared on the Great
White Way before, the 2013 Tony
Awards committee classified it as a
revival even though it had originally
premiered on television in 1957.

**NOMINATED TONYS
(ORIGINAL PRODUCTION)**
9

**WINNING TONYS
(ORIGINAL PRODUCTION)**
1

Ginger Rogers in a Hammered Stein

GLASS

chilled double
old-fashioned
(or a mule cup
if you have one)

8–10 mint leaves

¾ oz. ginger
syrup

2 oz. London dry
gin

1 oz. lemon
juice, freshly
squeezed

2 oz. ginger ale,
to top

GARNISH
mint sprig

SERVES 1 No, Ginger Rogers isn't related to Rodgers and Hammerstein composer Richard Rodgers—but their paths did intersect when Ginger Rogers appeared alongside Walter Pidgeon in the 1965 adaptation of *Cinderella*. Paying respects to this unexpected mash-up, the Ginger Rogers in a Hammered Stein breathes additional life into your hammered copper mugs traditionally held in reserve for those Dark 'n Stormy nights or Moscow Mules.

Cinderella was Rodgers and Hammerstein's only musical written for television, and its 1957 debut starred Julie Andrews. As part of the promotion for the live broadcast, Pepsi printed up five million four-page comic books to be sold with cartons of the drink in the weeks leading up to the airing. Although kinescopes of the initial broadcast exist, no original videotapes are known to survive so, when the successful London stage adaptation inspired CBS to bring the show back in 1965, Rogers's dance with a Rodgers and Hammerstein production became the canonical version. Over the next decade, the 1965 production aired eight more times, before Brandy became the first Black actress to play Cinderella on screen for the musical's 1997 adaptation. (The 2013 Broadway premiere of the show featured Laura Osnes in the title role, and later Carly Rae Jepsen and Keke Palmer.)

So raise a glass to your *Cinderella* of choice, and settle in for a lovely night of making the impossible possible.

Place all but one of the mint leaves into the small side of a shaker tin, add the ginger syrup, then bruise the leaves with a muddler or a spoon until you can smell the mint. Add the gin and lemon juice plus ice, then shake hard until the tin is fully frosted over. Fine-strain onto fresh ice, adding ginger ale and then a mint leaf for aroma.

Funny Girl

MUSIC BY
Jule Styne

BOOK BY
Isobel Lennart

LYRICS BY
Bob Merrill

BROADWAY OPENING
March 26, 1964
AT THE
Winter Garden Theatre

WEST END OPENING
April 13, 1966
AT THE
Prince of Wales Theatre

Fun Facts

Barbra Streisand is more celebrated for her film portrayal of Fanny Brice in the motion picture version of *Funny Girl*. Although she was nominated for a Tony Award for Best Actress for *Funny Girl* in 1964, she lost to Carol Channing, who was nominated for *Hello, Dolly!*

NOMINATED TONYS (ORIGINAL PRODUCTION)

8

GLASS

charged mug

2 oz. aged rum

2 tbsp. spiced
butter batter
(see recipe
next page)

5–6 oz. boiling
water

GARNISH
orange swath
studded with
whole cloves,
or a cinnamon
stick, or a little
fresh grated
nutmeg, or all
three

Don't Rum on My Parade

SERVES 1   Nobody was bringing around any clouds when Barbra Streisand marched her march out as Fanny Brice in the 1964 musical *Funny Girl*. Based on vaudeville and theatre star Brice's life, the musical marked Streisand's second—and final—bow on the Great White Way, securing her a Tony nomination for Best Actress in a Musical, and earning her two spots in the Grammy Hall of Fame. (These spots respectively came in 1998 for the ballad "People" and in 2004 for the musical's soundtrack.) *Funny Girl* has lived on in pop culture, with a notable film adaptation in which Streisand reprised her role opposite Omar Sharif, and with pop groups from the Supremes to the cast of the TV show *Glee* belting out iconic numbers like "People" and "Don't Rain on My Parade."

Life is like candy and the sun is all a ball of butter in this hot-buttered rum rendition sure to please people who need people! The secret to our recipe is in the made-ahead "batter." It's a mixture of butter, spice, and sweetness that, once prepared, combines near effortlessly with a little boiling water and a good shot of rum.

Combine the rum and butter-batter in the preheated mug, then carefully add 5 to 6 ounces of boiling water and stir until the butter has melted. Garnish and enjoy a great winter warmer.

ENCORE
Want to punch your hot-buttered rum up a little? A ¼ ounce of Cointreau or Galliano would be a welcome addition. Hot cider instead of hot water? Delicious!

138

Spiced Butter Batter

In a medium bowl combine all ingredients, then beat together until the sugar and spices are fully incorporated into the butter. While a hand mixer is great to have here, a fork and a little bit of persistence will get the job done. Once prepared, transfer to a resealable container and store refrigerated. Protected from heat and light, the "batter" will keep for up to a week.

1 stick slightly softened unsalted butter (Salted butter is fine, but then omit the pinch of salt below.)

½ cup brown sugar

1 tsp. ground allspice

1 tsp. ground nutmeg

1 tsp. ground cloves

1 tsp. vanilla extract

1 pinch salt

Singin' in the Rain

MUSIC BY
Nacio Herb Brown

LYRICS BY
Arthur Freed

BOOK BY
Adolph Green and Betty Comden

BROADWAY OPENING
July 2, 1985
AT THE
Gershwin Theatre

WEST END OPENING
June 30, 1983
AT THE
London Palladium

Fun Facts

The iconic "Singin' in the Rain" sequence featured a rain shower on stage.

NOMINATED TONYS
(ORIGINAL PRODUCTION)

2

Stay Up Lat(t)e, or the Good Foamin'

SERVES 1   The image of Don Lockwood tap-dancing in rain, blissfully unaware of the deluge since he's so in love, is iconic in the history of musicals. Although best remembered as the 1952 Gene Kelly flick, *Singin' in the Rain* did come to the Great White Way in 1985 after a run on the West End. The show was lukewarmly received by critics, however, who didn't think it lived up to the movie's original charm. Audiences seemed to agree, as it closed after only 367 shows. But songs like "Good Mornin'" and the title number are so immortal in the show-tune canon that it deserves a spot in our drink playbill.

Since *Singin' in the Rain* is a love letter to the history of cinema, this modern take on the espresso martini pairs perfectly with a late-night movie marathon of your favorite musical adaptations. As an extra dose of flair, consider adding a cocktail umbrella as a topper to the drink—your guests are free to abandon them as they see fit, but the addition of the unexpected garnish is sure to make 'em laugh. After all, you can't go wrong with physical prop comedy, as long as it's done with dignity. Always dignity.

Combine all ingredients except milk in your shaker, add 5 to 6 ice cubes, seal, and shake hard until the tin is cold to the touch. Strain, and if you've chosen to include it, add the steamed, foamed, or just regular old milk, then garnish by expressing the lemon peel, dropping the coffee beans, or sprinkling the ground coffee.

NOTE: While using an espresso vodka is a great elevated option for this cocktail, your go-to already-in-the-house vodka will be more than up to the task. For our vegan friends, oat milk is probably best.

GLASS

chilled coupe

2 oz. vodka

½ oz. coffee liqueur

1 oz. cold brew concentrate or espresso

½ oz. simple syrup

½ oz. frothed milk, optional

GARNISH
a few coffee beans, an expressed lemon twist, or a sprinkling of finely ground coffee are all wonderful

Les Misérables

MUSIC BY
Claude-Michel Schönberg

LYRICS BY
Alain Boublil and Jean-Marc Natel

BOOK BY
Claude-Michel Schönberg and Alain Boublil

BROADWAY OPENING
March 12, 1987
AT THE
Broadway Theatre

WEST END OPENING
October 8, 1985
AT THE
Barbican Theatre

Fun Facts

In a 2005 poll conducted by BBC Radio 2, *Les Mis* ranked as the most essential musical.

NOMINATED TONYS
(ORIGINAL PRODUCTION)
12

WINNING TONYS
(ORIGINAL PRODUCTION)
8

GLASS

toddy mug

---

6 oz. hot water,
plus more to
"charge" the
serving glass

2 oz. Campari

½ oz. Fernet

¾ oz. honey
simple syrup
(or ½ oz.
honey and a
little more hot
water)

½ oz. lemon juice

A pinch salt

GARNISH
expressed
lemon twist,
optional

One Drink More

SERVES 1 For our closing number at last call, we need an iconic musical to bring down the curtain. And *Les Misérables* fits the (play)bill. Based on the 1862 Victor Hugo novel of the same name, *Les Mis* first opened on the West End in 1985—where it is still the longest-running musical in West End history—and opened on Broadway two years later, where it remained until 2003. The original run was nominated for a then-record twelve Tony Awards. It has lived on in the hearts and minds of critics and audiences alike as one of the greatest musicals of all time.

This hot toddy variant also serves as a brilliant digestif to close out a night of carousing (or storming the barricades). It will serve as a welcome comfort to those like Jean Valjean who have spent one too many nights in the cold, and just one sip of it will make many shout "Vive la France!"

Charge toddy mug with extra hot water for a minute or two to warm it up. Discard the water. Combine cocktail ingredients and additional 6 oz. hot water directly in the mug (don't forget the salt!), stir to combine. Garnish with expressed lemon peel if desired and serve immediately.

CLOSE
CURTAIN

ĪNDEX

ABOUT THE AUTHORS

MICHAEL GOFF's culinary approach to bartending has brought him to work at cutting-edge bars like Mother of Pearl and the *New York Times* three-starred Le Crocodile in New York City's Lower East Side and Williamsburg neighborhoods, respectively. These days he can be found slinging handcrafted drinks and putting smiles on faces all over Manhattan.

A lifelong theatre fan, **RONNIE ALVARADO** has been belting out show tunes (off-key) since seeing her first Broadway show, *Beauty and the Beast*. She works in book publishing and lives in New York City.

MICHAEL ANDERSEN is a frequent guest on the immersive theatre podcast *No Proscenium*, where he obsesses over everything from escape room musicals to weekend-long musical-themed puzzle hunts. Sometimes, he even makes the trek from Jersey City to catch more traditional Broadway fare.